Mercantile Bombay

T0299856

This volume reclaims Mumbai's legacy as a global financial centre of the 19th to the first half of the 20th century. It shows how Mumbai, or erstwhile Bombay, once served as a central node in global networks of trade, finance, commercial institutions and most importantly trading communities. In doing so it highlights that this city more than any other Indian city still possesses all these virtuous elements making it an appropriate location for a financial special economic zone (SEZ) – an idea shelved temporarily.

The book explores how the city flourished in its heyday as a trading, financial, commercial and manufacturing hub in a globalised colonial world. While the city's importance as a nodal financial hub in the global economy ebbed post India's Independence and the Second World War, the multi-cultural city found renewed importance following the forex crisis of 1991. Institutions (the RBI, SEBI and State Bank of India headquarters), capacities, experiences, communities and talent centred in Mumbai revived its position, while managing the transition to a more open economy. Though Mumbai is not yet an international financial centre (financial SEZ) like London, New York, Dubai, Singapore, Hong Kong, this volume explores why it has all the essential elements to become one today, and looks at the city as a trading city, a global financial centre, and a city of enterprise.

An introspective read on India's financial capital, this volume will be essential for scholars and researchers of economics, business studies and commerce. It will be of great interest to policy makers, city-headquartered business houses, financial institutions and its people.

Sifra Lentin is a Mumbai-based author and Bombay History Fellow at Gateway House: Indian Council on Global Relations, a foreign policy think tank in Mumbai, India. *Mercantile Bombay: A Journey of Trade, Finance and Enterprise* is her first book on Bombay. Other books written by her are: the Indian Navy's Western Fleet coffee-table book *A Salute to the Sword Arm – a Photo Essay on the Western Fleet* (April 2007), and more recently *Our Legacy: The Dwarkadas Family of Bombay* (March 2018).

The Gateway House Guide to India in the 2020s

Series Editor: **Manjeet Kripalani**, *co-founder*
Gateway House: Indian Council on Global Relations

The Gateway House Guide to India in the 2020s explores the connections between India's globalist past to the strengths it has developed as it steps into the future, starting with the decade of the 2020s. The volumes in this series discuss a wide range of topics, which include solutions for energy independence and environmental preservation, exposition of the new frontiers in space and technology, India's trade networks, security, foreign policies and international relations. Furthermore, the series examines the embedded trading and entrepreneurial communities which are coming together to influence global agenda-setting and institution-building through platforms like the G20 and UN Security Council, where India will take leadership roles in this decade, in the post-COVID-19 pandemic world.

This series appeals to an international audience, and is directed to policymakers, think tanks, bureaucrats and professionals working in the area of politics; scholars and researchers of political science, international relations, foreign policy, world economy, politics and technology, Asian politics, South Asia studies and contemporary history; and students and the general reader, seeking an understanding of what will drive India's positioning in world affairs.

Mercantile Bombay
A Journey of Trade, Finance and Enterprise
Sifra Lentin

India and the Changing Geopolitics of Oil
Amit Bhandari

For more information about this series, please visit: https://www.routledge.com/The-Gateway-House-Guide-to-India-in-the-2020s/book-series/GHGI20

Mercantile Bombay

A Journey of Trade, Finance and Enterprise

Sifra Lentin

Routledge
Taylor & Francis Group

LONDON AND NEW YORK

First published 2022
by Routledge
2 Park Square, Milton Park, Abingdon, Oxon OX14 4RN

and by Routledge
605 Third Avenue, New York, NY 10158

Routledge is an imprint of the Taylor & Francis Group, an informa business

© 2022 Gateway House: Indian Council on Global Relations

The right of Sifra Lentin to be identified as author of this work has been asserted by her in accordance with sections 77 and 78 of the Copyright, Designs and Patents Act 1988.

All rights reserved. No part of this book may be reprinted or reproduced or utilised in any form or by any electronic, mechanical, or other means, now known or hereafter invented, including photocopying and recording, or in any information storage or retrieval system, without permission in writing from the publishers.

Trademark notice: Product or corporate names may be trademarks or registered trademarks, and are used only for identification and explanation without intent to infringe.

British Library Cataloguing-in-Publication Data
A catalogue record for this book is available from the British Library

Library of Congress Cataloging-in-Publication Data
A catalog record has been requested for this book

ISBN: 978-0-367-77418-9 (hbk)
ISBN: 978-1-032-02323-6 (pbk)
ISBN: 978-1-003-18289-4 (ebk)

DOI: 10.4324/9781003182894

Typeset in Times New Roman
by MPS Limited, Dehradun

To my late father Nissim Samuel who was such a great story-teller and instilled in me a love for the written word.

Contents

Figures

Tables

Acknowledgements

There are many, many people who have contributed to this book in ways big and small, and in times far and near.

I would like to thank Manjeet Kripalani and Ambassador Neelam Deo both founder directors of Gateway House: Indian Council on Global Relations for believing that a history fellow would be a perfect fit for a foreign policy think tank! It is this belief and my still ongoing fellowship at Gateway House – nine years and counting – that has resulted in my unique foreign policy perspective on the history of Bombay, something I share in this book. My colleagues – past and present – at Gateway House have helped sharpen my understanding of geopolitics, geoeconomics, science and technology, global and internal circulations of people, and how culture and faith transcend hard borders.

More particularly, I would like to thank my dear friends Deepak Rao and Dr Bazil Shaikh. Rao is an old friend since the time I penned my weekly column *Vintage Bombay,* later *Vintage Mumbai* after the city was renamed in 1995. He has been my go-to person for all things Bombay and even today nudges me in the right direction every time I meet a dead-end. Shaikh is a friend from my early days at Gateway House and is a master on the history of the Bombay mint, Indian currency and banking. I am glad we met when we did because our conversations have deepened my understanding of this wonderful city built for trade and commerce. Cdr. Mohan Narayan, late Dr (Prof) Arunachalam and late Vice Admiral Manohar Awati, together curated some of the finest lectures and maritime history courses under the auspices of the Western Naval Command's Maritime History Society – I never missed a single lecture or course then. They made me view Bombay from the sea.

I am most grateful to my interviewees, some of who I have named but not all, who have shared their knowledge and experiences and made the time to answer all my questions patiently. There were at least 15 diplomats that I interviewed who all made the effort to look up the history of their

Missions in Bombay *before* meeting me. Some shared books and all of them their valuable insights on the shared history between Bombay and their countries.

Asha Rani, our librarian at Gateway House is an incredible resource for any researcher, often finding online papers and books that I had missed.

Introduction

The aim of this book is to *reclaim* Mumbai's[1] legacy as a global financial centre, by highlighting all the virtuous elements it still possesses: global networks of trade, finance, institutions and most importantly trading communities, whose presence in the city goes back to its heydays as a trading, financial, commercial and manufacturing hub, albeit in a globalised colonial world. These networks that were established during the 19th century were dismantled and reconfigured after the Second World War, leaving Bombay out of the ebb and flow of international finance and trade, also partly due to newly independent India's own socialist-inspired, insular economic policies.

After the forex crisis of 1991, Bombay (as it was called till 1995) reclaimed its centricity in India, not just because it was the country's financial capital but because it had the institutions (the Reserve Bank of India [RBI], Securities and Exchange Board of India [SEBI] and State Bank of India headquarters), capacities, experience, communities, and talent to manage this transition. India opened up its capital markets to foreign investors, offered its manufacturing to foreign companies, and staggered the Indian Rupee into free float (on current but not yet fully on capital account) into the international forex markets.

Twenty-first-century Mumbai is a financial centre and multicultural hub, like London, New York, Dubai, Singapore, Hong Kong. Unlike them, however, it is **not** an international financial centre (IFC; financial special economic zone [SEZ]) though it has all the virtuous elements to become one. These are embedded in its legacy of having been a central node in a global colonial network of trade, commerce, and credit from the 1870s to the early decades of the 20th century.

Unlike other Bombay books, *Mercantile Bombay: A Journey of Trade, Finance and Enterprise* approaches the mercantile history of the city as a vital and living legacy. It does this in the following ways:

DOI: 10.4324/9781003182894-101

For one, it focuses on Bombay the trading city, where communities near and far thronged, enriching it and themselves financially, culturally and faithfully. The institutional, cultural and religious footprints of these migrant and émigré communities are still discernable. For example, all the big Lohana business families of East Africa have offices in the city, not just for trade but for sourcing manpower, just as they did a 150 years ago.

Secondly, it draws out the history of Bombay as a global financial centre in the 19th and early 20th centuries, whilst highlighting the return of multinational businesses and the consulates that once had a presence in the city. This indicates the centrality of 21st-century Mumbai for tapping into a fast-expanding Indian economy, just as it once did in the past. For nearly two centuries, Bombay, as it was then, was a global financial centre and was commonly referred to as 'the most important city east of Suez'. The colonial Indian rupee was a multilateral trading currency, and infrastructure projects like the Great Indian Peninsula Railway (today's Central Railway) raised rupee-based bonds on the London Stock Exchange. It was well-integrated into global supply chains, markets, and credit networks, and its reintegration today is exemplified by the very same foreign consulates, foreign banks and their agents, even ambassadors for cities like Hamburg, which had a Bombay consulate as early as 1844, foreign investment banks and funds, setting up offices in Mumbai. They are here to invest in the India story or seeking reverse investments from Indian companies into their economies via Mumbai.

Lastly, all the aforementioned would not be possible without Bombay being a city of enterprise. Bombay's merchants have always seized opportunity whether in the city or elsewhere. In the early 19th century, when Bengal and its port of Calcutta dominated the opium trade to China, largely controlled by the English East India Company (EEIC), Bombay's merchants overtook it by sourcing the cheaper variant of this drug from Princely Kingdoms and bypassing Bombay port itself, in order to ship this drug to Canton. It was only when the Bombay presidency government, realising it would lose valuable revenue, permitted opium exports through Bombay port.

In order to highlight what once was and can be Mumbai's role yet again in the 21st century, Chapters 1 and 2 provide the context – what made Bombay so successful – whilst the remaining four chapters deal with specifics like the indigenous bankers who were attracted to the opportunities in the city and commercial communities who created and built upon overseas networks in the Middle-East, East Africa and the Far East.

Chapter 1 – 'How Bombay became the confluence of commerce and culture' – contextualises the history of the original seven islands **before** the advent of the EEIC. The Islands then had a sparse local trade and its isolated anchorages were a cover for pirates and regional powers.. It singles out the critical role of the Bombay Marine – the EEIC's marine force – not just in securing the island city from its foes but also in using the seas as a bridgehead to expand Bombay's sphere of political influence and territories to create a Presidency named after this city. Pertinently, this once rag-tag force of European deserters and ex-prisoners (pardoned only if they served in this marine force) is the forerunner of the Indian Navy's blue water Western Fleet headquartered in the city.

Chapter 2 – 'The port and the city' – highlights how pivotal the city's port and harbour is to the success of Mumbai just as it was to the growth and success of Bombay 200 years ago. Even today, Bombay Port and JNPT handle 17.4%[2] of India's total cargo traffic. This chapter explores how changes in shipping technology in the 18th century favoured sheltered open sea harbours like Bombay's, as against traditional riverine ports, like Surat. Further, the trade that the Company's marine force secured, whether the smuggling of opium to China, cotton exports, teak, and for a time the triangular East African ivory trade (of which Bombay port was an important transit point), secured the city's place as an international trading hub – for exports and imports, transshipment, and ship-building and repairs. The learnings from this chapter is that some of the greatest port cities in the world, like Hong Kong and Bombay, have originally been just rocky outcrops BUT a strategic location on main shipping routes, a strong navy, enterprising trading communities, and the acquisition of a hinterland, all these are necessary ingredients for success.

Chapter 3 – 'Migrants in the city and their overseas networks' – deals with waves of migrations – old and new. Its focus is on why trading communities chose the city; where they settled; how they added to Bombay's trade, commerce, and native banking services, and their community ecosystems – places of worship, schools, housing, charities and so on. This chapter covers the migration of communities that are well-known in the Middle East and East Africa trade, like the Bhatia, Khoja and Bohra immigrants, and whose histories broadly reflect that of other trading migrant communities like the Lohana, Parsi and Patidar. The focus of this chapter is that overseas networks transcend national borders and the circulations of people from India's west coast often pre-dated the settlement of these communities in Bombay.

Chapter 4 – 'Émigrés of the Bombay Presidency' – covers three major regions of trade with Bombay – the Persian Gulf, South Central Asia and the Far East. Unlike internal migrants, the presence of these émigré communities is residual in the city today. In delineating the early history of trade with these regions, the pioneers who settled here, the formation of a sustainable community and their religious-cultural ecosystem, and the importance of their combined contributions to the city are what highlight the importance of the overseas trade networks that foreign diaspora communities bring with them. Some communities like the Baghdadi Jews became internationally prominent, often making the transition into manufacturing, and expanding globally outwards from the city. Newer expatriate communities, like the Japanese, most of who arrived along with the big Japanese trading companies, added their own unique overlay to Mumbai's multicultural ecosystem, some of which are still visible in the city today.

Chapter 5 – 'Finance, *desi* and *videshi*' – is kaleidoscopic in nature. It begins with how the Company's Bombay rupee insinuated itself into Indian Ocean trading networks by riding on the credibility of the Mughal silver rupee. Unlike the Mughal rupee, the Bombay rupee was probably the first currency denomination ever to be popularised among locals in regions of the Middle East and East Africa through the overseas networks of Indian merchant communities. The success of the *Hundi*, a native bill of exchange, and its variants, in facilitating both domestic and international trade (Middle East, East Africa, Central Asia) and its credit needs, underscores one of the reasons why modern banking made a relatively late arrival in Bombay with the setting up of the Bank of Bombay in 1840. There was one major drawback to the *Hundi*, it could not be used in Great Britain, Europe, the Americas and China. The EEIC used the *Hundi* to raise money for its local trade but it sent money to London using the instrument of Council and Reverse Council Bills, a system of transfer of funds that ensured a monopoly in forex for themselves and the Agency Houses. Forex banking was first attempted in the city through the initiative of Bombay's resident merchant community – local and émigré – in 1842. By the time India's central bank opened its headquarters in Bombay on 1 April 1935, the city's banking services were already well-integrated into global credit networks. The setting up of a central bank for India and the first such institution of its kind in Asia underscores that Bombay was not just the financial capital for British India then, but its influence encompassed the regions in both the northern Arabian Sea and the Bay of Bengal.

Chapter 6 – 'Mercantile and a multicultural city'– is the soft diplomacy element in the book – Hindi Films and the Bombay Progressive Artists – and the émigrés who made valuable contributions to it. This overt intervention by European émigrés overlaps with 'Between the Wars: Nationalism & Global Influences', which narrates the heightened Indian nationalism during the inter-war years, which was accompanied with a shift from British influence to other countries and ideologies, often brought about by refugees who made the city their temporary home. The other aspect of this expat element in the city were the foreign diplomatic corp., who played a vital part in the cultural life of the city. The focus of this chapter is how overseas influences, however brief, can integrate a city with global trends – whether in arts, films, ideologies, science or literature – making it international in its outlook.

This book in the final count draws together all the virtuous elements in Mumbai's history that played a key role in its commercial success in the past, and can be leveraged in its present by India's policy makers, Mumbai's urban planners and the city government. The histories and oral histories woven into the narrative of *Mercantile Bombay: A Journey of Trade, Finance and Enterprise* demonstrates that there is a part of almost every region and people of the world that have at some point played a role, however small, in the history of this city by the sea.

Sifra Lentin
October 2021

Notes

1 The name Mumbai is used when referring to the city post 1995, the year it was renamed. For the purposes of this book Bombay is used when referring to the colonial history of the city - both Portuguese and English.
2 http://shipmin.gov.in/sites/default/files/Major%20Ports%20november%202020.pdf.

1 How Bombay became the confluence of commerce and culture

Five hundred years ago, the seven islands of Bombay – Colaba & Old Woman's Island, Bombay, Worli, Parel, Mahim, Mazagaon and Sion itself – till they were raised from the seas through reclamations, were non-descript, rocky outcrops separated from each other during low tide by shallow marshy creeks. The largest in this seven-island group was the H-shaped island of Bombay (locally known as *Mumbaaiee* after the Island's patron goddess *Mumbadevi*). There was nothing to commend the islands as an attractive destination for trade, commerce and enterprise, except for the fact that it was located on an arterial Indian Ocean shipping route leading to the pepper coast of Malabar and beyond to the spice islands of South East Asia, and then onwards to the Far East – China and Japan. The same route on its westward trajectory would take you to the Persian Gulf region – with its ports of Muscat, Basra and Gombroon (Bandar Abbas) – the Red Sea ports and the coast of East Africa.

Though Bombay was geo-strategically well situated, it was only when the Islands were leased by the English Crown on 27 March 1668 to the world's first joint stock company – the *Governor and Company of Merchants of London trading into the East Indies*[1] (in short, the EEIC) that an effort was made to develop the islands expansive open sea, sheltered, harbour into a port city. The sole objective being the acceleration of English trade in the North Arabian Sea.

There were many reasons why the Islands were not viewed favourably for development earlier, although Portuguese authorities in India did realise its potential, even if belatedly.

First, Bombay possessed an 'open' sea harbour, albeit a sheltered one sandwiched between its hilly eastern foreshore and the mainland. Smaller sailing ships with a shallow draught – a norm during the medieval and early modern period – favoured the shelter provided by riverine harbours especially during the monsoon months. Its harbour

DOI: 10.4324/9781003182894-1

anchorages were known for centuries to local and intra-Asian ship-ping. The foremost port in the vicinity of Bombay was the medieval Mughal port of Surat on the River Tapi.[2] It was only when the con-struction of larger sailing ships with a deeper draught became the norm, that the advantages of Bombay's sheltered open sea harbour drew the attention of the Surat factors (merchants) of the EEIC. Their reason was simple. Bombay had the advantage of proximity to as well as re-lative distance from – the contentious politics and security issues in – the port city of Surat. This made it an ideal location for an auxiliary out-post, a fact pointed out by the EEIC Surat council as early as 1652 in a letter to the then British head of state Oliver Cromwell.

Second, the Islands faced insurmountable geo-economic challenges. It did **not** possess a hinterland – a prerequisite for any port city. A hinterland performs two functions: it is a source of surplus exportable goods and commodities, and it is a market for imports. The lack of a productive hinterland under its control and sphere of political influ-ence was a practical difficulty Bombay faced. Bombay islands in 1665 – when the English expeditionary force wrested control of them from the Portuguese – were located at the remote southern tip of a larger and more productive island, Salsette (Sashti).

Salsette was not only controlled by the adversarial Portuguese but it also was traditionally a source of basic supplies – like milch livestock – for Bombay. Unlike Portuguese-occupied Salsette, Bombay islands did not produce any saleable surplus besides dried fish, salt, coconuts and coir. Salsette was also for centuries Bombay's linkage with land and sea-based trading routes. Since ancient times, the ports of Salsette, one of them Thana (famous for its Roman trade dating to the 4th century), were the terminal points of the southern branch of the ancient Silk Route.

Third, and related to Bombay's hinterland challenges, was that the H-shaped island of Bombay was not a secure location for a port as it was notorious as a 'pirate's isle'. The islands – a part of an archipelago of 25 islands referred to by Ptolemy in the 1st century as Heptanesia – were located on the North Konkan Coast, a region that suffered from endemic piracy. Piracy on the Subcontinent's west coast was sup-pressed by colonial navies only as late as the early 19th century.

The only remnant in Bombay of this buccaneering past is Malabar Hill, among the most expensive real estate in the city today. Its name points to the hill's history. This hill – a 280-foot basaltic formation fronting the open Arabian Sea – is named incongruently after the 'original' Malabar (coast),[3] a region hundreds of kilometres to its south and once notorious as home to the Malabar pirates. During the

9th –13th centuries, when the islands were ruled by the Silāharā chieftains of the Konkan, the famous Venetian merchant traveller Marco Polo[4] wrote in his *The Travels of Marco Polo* of the 'sea-robbers and corsairs' in Bombay harbour at the close of the 13th century. The account that quotes Marco Polo specifically refers to Malabar Hill: 'one of the many bands of pirates who harassed the coast-trade from Gujarat southwards and later gave their name to the hill and promontory of our island' (Edwardes 1909).

Bombay was because of the aforementioned reasons an untenable location for a port city. This fact is borne out by history too. It took close to 100 years for the city to become a viable alternative to the Mughal port of Surat – in spite of Surat's irreversible decline after the death of Mughal Emperor Aurangzeb in 1707.

But Bombay's time had arrived. A key foundational event in Bombay's geo-strategic and political history was the shifting of the Company's naval force from Surat to Bombay in 1687 – also the year when Bombay became the headquarters of the Company on the Subcontinent's west coast.

This move was triggered by insecurity at Surat and the political harassment of the Company's trade and merchants there. But it proved a fortuitous one. It gave the new governor and council at Bombay an opportunity to establish maritime domain control and awareness not only of Bombay's territorial seas but also in littoral regions overseas. It was this EEIC navy – renamed the Bombay Marine in 1687 itself – which through its many subsequent *avatars as* the Indian Navy, Royal Indian Navy,[5] Royal Indian Marine, independent India's Indian Navy, and finally India's Western Fleet (still headquartered in Mumbai) not just protected Bombay and its trade BUT also projected the city's naval power overseas and acted as a bridgehead for territorial expansion. It is to the early successes of the Bombay Marine *before* it began recruiting in the early 19th century the very same locals from the North Konkan Coast it had once fought, that one sees Bombay the global port and international financial and commercial city taking shape (Figure 1.1).

The Bombay Marine: security, armed diplomacy and territorial acquisitions

The Bombay Marine and its hydrographic surveys of the Arabian Sea can be largely credited with the increasing sphere of influence and territory of the Presidency of Bombay (1708–1936).[6] The city was designated in 1708 as the capital of a presidency named after it – which

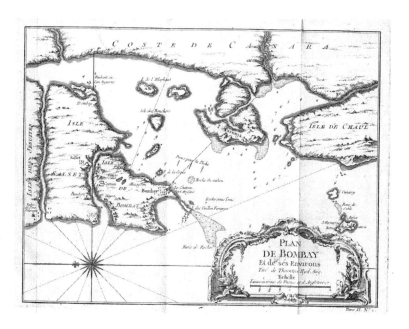

Figure 1.1 An early 18th C map of Bombay and the harbour islands.

Source: From the collection of Jehangir Sorabjee.

brought all the Company's outposts on the subcontinent's west coast under its purview. This made its governor and council answerable only to the Court of Directors in London, but only initially. In 1773, the Presidency of Bombay was subordinated to Bengal.[7]

It was the city's Bombay Marine that established and secured the EEIC's interests not only on the subcontinent's west coast but often on its east coast too, making it the Company's primary naval force. It often teamed up with the Royal Navy on major expeditions and anti-slavery and anti-piracy patrols in the Indian Ocean. This naval force traces its roots to the original marine service consisting of a squadron of four ships – *Dragon, Hoseander, James* and *Solomon* – that voyaged from England to Surat under the command of Captain Thomas Best to establish an English factory (a trading establishment in a foreign port) in Surat.

This Squadron arrived on 5 September 1612, which is regarded as the founding date of the Bombay Marine. Earlier attempts had been made by the Company – from 1601 to 1608 – to establish a factory at Surat but they failed because of Portuguese naval resistance at Surat.

In a naval battle at Swally – downriver from Surat – in 1612, the English squadron finally overcame the Portuguese fleet to establish English naval supremacy, at least for the time being. This victory enabled Sir Thomas Roe's mission of 1615–1618, envoy of King James II, to make his way to Delhi to acquire the Mughal Emperor's *firman* for trading privileges. In its early years, the Bombay Marine's main duties revolved around securing the trade of the EEIC against the dangers of piracy and attacks by other local rulers and European competitors, like the Portuguese, the Dutch and the French.

It was only after its headquarters were relocated to Bombay, did the role of the Bombay Marine evolve and become more calibrated. Due to the compulsions of trade in these early years, the Company had to use the Bombay Marine to secure its political and economic interests especially in regions like Kutch, Kathiawar, Gulf of Cambay (Khambhat), Canara, Malabar and the Gulf, from where it sourced its goods.

The Marine proved effective – as a naval fleet with a corps of soldiers who could fight on land and sea. They packed the hardest punch with the minimum number of men. This was a difficult feat to achieve, given the endemic disciplinary problems this Marine force faced. The officers as well as sailors of the Marine were regularly recruited from England – a motley group, many of who had been released from jails in England and given their freedom after they promised to serve in the Bombay Marine. No one else was willing to serve in Bombay preferring Calcutta, as the lifetime of an Englishman here was often no more than two monsoons. A large number of recruits were also renegades from English and European merchant vessels. All this translated into problems like drunkenness, fights and unruliness in the numerous taverns in the fortified town of Bombay. Despite the waywardness of its crews in the 17th and 18th centuries, the Marine played a critical role in securing and expanding the trade, territories and influence of this city.

Staking out territorial seas: *mare liberum* versus *mare clausum*

Most contemporary historians agree that piracy in the Indian Ocean region was a vocation that most coastal communities took to, often with the explicit support of their chief or king. This was the case with most, so called, piratical people, whether the fierce Malabar pirates who owed their loyalty to the Zamorin of Calicut or the various bands of Kutch pirates, the Vaddellas and Sungannas, the Sanganians of Beyt and Dwarka, the Koli rovers of Gujarat, the Warrals of Diu and Gogo (Gogha) all to the north of Bombay. To the south of the island the Mallwans (60 miles north of Goa), various Maratha coastal communities near Sawantwadi and Vengurla also took to piracy (Maloni 1992) (Biddulp n.d.). Then there were the Muscat Arabs and the Qawasim tribes of the Persian Gulf, who roamed the Gulf and the north Arabian Sea.

In Indian pre-colonial littoral communities as elsewhere in the Indian Ocean, the concept of 'territorial seas' or 'maritime boundaries' as envisaged in the West did not exist. It was only when the Portuguese entered in the 15th century, this closely knit trading world dominated by Arab shipping, that an awareness of 'territorial' seas took root and also its potential as a source of revenue. The Portuguese enforced a system of a paid *cartaz* (pass) for any ship passing through seas adjacent to their colonial outposts. It is pertinent that the Portuguese empire in the Indian Ocean was dominated by a string of coastal fortresses, while Indian rulers then traditionally looked landwards.

This divergence between the European perspective of 'territorial seas' (*mare clausum*) and the Indian Ocean norm of 'open seas' (*mare liberum*) led to a clash between the European companies and native kingdoms and tribes' resident on the coast, during the 16th to the early 19th centuries. The problem for Bombay began when Indian coastal potentates – like the Maratha admirals, the Angres, who took up the baton from Chhatrapati Shivaji of developing a strong Maratha navy (and succeeded!) to patrol their seas, enforce their *dastak* (pass) and convoy their coastal trade – began flexing their naval power in the environs of Bombay.

Before the rise of the Angres, the Sidi (Abyssinian) admirals of the Mughals were a much-dreaded nuisance to the town and island of Bombay throughout the late 17th century (see Table 1.1), wreaking havoc on its trade, destroying lives and properties and on numerous occasions leaving behind an outbreak of plague, almost annually, as they used the islands as a base to launch their attacks on the Maratha *kurlahs* (land and villages like Panvel and Pen) on the mainland to the east of Bombay harbour. During Shivaji's time, the Marathas and Sidis would clash in the harbour itself. But as can be seen from Table 1.1, Sidi power began declining with the decline of Mughal power after 1707. More often thereafter, the Company at Bombay began to support them in order to balance the growing power of the Marathas and their admirals, the Angres.

The writ of Kanhoji Angre: *mare clausum*

Never in the history of Bombay were its merchants so terrorised by the depredations of piracy, as they were during the reign of Kanhoji Angre

Table 1.1 List of major Bombay Marine actions and skirmishes in and near
Bombay's coastal waters.

Year	Location	Conflict
1658–1659	Sidi forts Danda-Rajpuri	Failed attempt by Bombay Marine
1672	Maratha King Shivaji attempts to fortify Kenery island (Khanderi) at the mouth of Bombay harbour	Bombay Marine thwart this first attempt
1673	7 Dutch ships threaten Bombay	Failed attempt as Shivaji refuses to help them
1672–1674 1677–1682 March 1683	Sidi Fleets winter during monsoon months in Bombay harbour near Mazagaon island.	Bombay town and islands subject to raids by the Sidis
15 February 1689–22 June 1690	Sidi Admiral Yakut Khan and his forces occupy the seven islands of Bombay	Sidis terrorise the people of Bombay and only leave after they are ordered to do so by Mughal Emperor Aurangzeb
1691	Sidi Fleet reappears on Mazagaon island	This time they are beaten back by a local militia of Koli fishermen who are lead by a Parsi – Rustom Dorab – who is honoured by the hereditary title `Patell' or headman
1712	Maratha Admiral Kanoji Angre makes his first attack on shipping in Bombay harbour	He is successful as he gets a ransom from Bombay's citizens of Rs 30,000 to release hostages
1719	Bombay Marine attack on the Angre occupied Kenery island (Khanderi)	Attempt fails

(Continued)

Table 1.1 (Continued)

Year	Location	Conflict
1720–1722	In the waters off Portuguese occupied Bandora (Bandra) in the north of Bombay	Skirmishes between Bombay Marine and the Portuguese over demands for payment of *Cartaz* to enable passage through Portuguese coastal waters
1722	Attack on Maratha Admiral Kanoji Agre at Kulaba, south of Bombay harbour	Three Bombay Marine ships involved but the attack fails
1727	Capture of ships in Bombay Harbour by Angre	English ship Derby, and many Dutch and French vessels captured
1738/1739	Kanoji Angre's son Manaji captures the harbour islands of Karanja and Elephanta	Threatens shipping in the harbour
1756	Joint attack by the English, Portuguese and Maratha Peshwa Balaji Baji Rao (Nanasaheb) on the Sea Fortress of Gheria, stronghold of Tulaji Angre	The success of this attack led by the Bombay Marine ships secures the North Konkan Coast for the EEIC

over the North Konkan seas. British chronicles of the time branded Kanhoji as the *Pyrate Angria* whose attacks on the shipping of the city were so great that it warranted a petition by the native merchants of Bombay to the newly appointed president for Bombay and Governor Charles Boone (1715–1722) to put an end to the menace of Angre[8] (Edwardes Vol. 2 1909).

Kanhoji Angre is consistently referred to as a pirate in all British narratives, ranging from the old Bombay gazetteers to Clement Downing's *The Compendious History of the Indian Wars* (1737) that details the first joint anti-piracy mission – launched from the city to hunt down Kanhoji's descendants – by the Royal Navy and Bombay Marine. Downing was part of this mission and its chronicler (Downing 1737).

Today the viewpoint of colonial narratives has been revised particularly by the Indian Navy. Kanhoji Angre is considered to be the first
Maratha admiral who succeeded in enforcing his *dastak* (pass) on
foreign ships traversing through his territorial seas.

Kanhoji is very important to the history of Bombay and even after
his death in 1729 his descendants implemented his writ of closed seas.
This continued till the historic land-sea Battle of Gheria (1756), when
the Maratha Peshwa Balaji Baji Rao (Nanasaheb), fearing the power
of his own admiral, helped the British in overcoming Tulaji Angre.
This put an end to the 54-year-old reign of terror by the Angres on
Bombay's merchant community and trade.

The strategic genius of Kanhoji Angre is enshrined in Indian naval
lore and the naval base (formerly HMIS Dalhousie) behind the Old
Town Hall (the Central and Asiatic Society Library at Horniman
Circle in Fort) has been rechristened INS Angre on 15 September 1951
(Indian Navy n.d.). Ironically, INS Angre was once the old Bombay
Castle (before it the Portuguese *Quinta* or manor) and the headquarters of the EEIC and its navy – Bombay Marine – who contended
with the Agres' over maritime domain control in and near Bombay's
territorial waters.[9]

Kanhoji Angre is relevant today for the following reasons.
(Malgaonkar 1981)

One, he was a naval strategist who highlighted the susceptibility of the
island city to attacks from the sea. This has a particularly strong re-
sonance after the recent 26 November 2008 terrorist attack on Mumbai,
because Pakistan-trained terrorists used the Karachi–Mumbai sea route
to land at various points on the city's seaboard in order to carry out
their terror attack (Lentin 2013).

Very early in his career, Kanhoji Angre controlled the south-west
entry into Bombay harbour. This approach into the harbour (its main
shipping channel) has two little islands called Kenery (Khanderi) and
Henery (Undheri). Both islands are today part of Mumbai harbour.
Later, in 1739, Agre's son Manaji, captured and occupied the islands
of Karanja (till recently home to the Indian Naval War College) and
Elephanta (both situated in Bombay harbour). They too wreaked
havoc on shipping in the harbour by strategically encircling the island
city from the south-west approach and the east (harbour side).[10] The
north approach into Bombay was manned by Bassein (today's Vasai)
Fort that was then under Maratha rule.

Second, because of the strategic genius of the Angres, they effectively demonstrated that superior naval technology couldn't beat a
well-manned fleet of smaller *grabs (galbats)*, *ghurabs* and *pals* (all

coastal boats), plying close to their coastal forts, which were provided covering fire from landwards during an attack. The strategy was simple: any merchantman or naval ship not carrying the admiral's *dastak* to ply in Maratha coastal waters would be captured for ransom. The territorial seas of the Angres extended from the mainland across from Bombay harbour, with the exception of a few Sidi enclaves, right up to Vengurla, just short of Portuguese-ruled Goa.

According to current Indian naval thinking, the Marathas simply took their cue from the Portuguese, an alien European power who were the first European power to enforce their *cartaz* (pass) in Indian waters. Now the importance of territorial seas is well-established under the *United Nations Convention on the Law of the Seas* (UNCLOS), but 200 years ago, the Maratha admirals were the first Indian rulers to successfully enforce *mare clausum* or closed seas in this region.

Joint anti-piracy missions by the Royal Navy and Bombay Marine

The need to keep shipping lanes free of piracy, particularly the strategic energy corridors with Africa and West Asia, has made the north Arabian Sea the most patrolled waters in the world today.

This resonates with the anti-piracy missions sent from Bombay to weed out piracy in this same region. In the 17th and 18th centuries, it was the European privateers from the Caribbean islands and America who roamed these waters when they crossed over from the Atlantic Ocean, raised the 'Jolly Roger' somewhere off the West Coast of Africa and entered the Indian Ocean to prey on the annual Mughal Red Sea Fleet headed towards Jiddah (Jeddah) for the Haj market.

Privateers formed an informal navy, with crews and ships, and assisted their country's navy during a war. They were given letters of marque (a government license) by their regent, which permitted them to attack, capture and plunder ships belonging to the enemy. It was these privateers who doubled up as pirates during periods of peace, and roamed the seas attacking merchant shipping. Indian merchant ships heaving with goods and pilgrims for the annual market that took place during the Haj to Mecca and Medina on the Arabian Peninsula were easy prey for European pirates somewhere off the coast of Socotra Island before they entered the Red Sea.

The voluminous correspondence by the merchants of the Company, which make up the *Surat Factory Records* (English East India Company n.d.), are replete with not just the depredations of European piracy but also the backlash from the local merchant community of

Surat on the European merchants based there. The problem was that the local people of Surat could not distinguish between the Europeans and the pirates: they were all 'hat-wearing' and white-skinned. They were not exactly off-the-mark either, as many Europeans who headed to the East and Far East in the employment of the European companies often turned renegade, either becoming pirates or interlopers [11] or both in the transoceanic trade of the Companies.

Of particular note was the plunder off the coast of Bombay of Mughal Emperor Aurangzeb's ship the *Ganj Sawai (Gunsway)*, by the pirate Henry Every in 1695. The local population were outraged not just at the plunder of the imperial Haj ship but the abduction of the Sayyidi women (from the priestly class) who were on board, for the voyage from Surat to Jiddah for the annual Haj.

The concept of 'convoying' the annual Red Sea Haj fleet with European naval warships (English and Dutch) was implemented as a compromise soon after this incident (Das Gupta n.d.). Though convoying assuaged the feelings of local merchants, the incidents of piracy did not reduce.

In Bombay, the first real effort to attack pirate enclaves was made during the governorship of Charles Boone. The governor himself with the Bombay Marine tried to dislodge Kanhoji from the immediate precinct of Bombay, by attacking his fortress at Kenery and Kolaba. It was also during Boone's tenure that the first joint anti-piracy mission was undertaken by the Royal Navy and the Bombay Marine against the European pirates (Captain Seegar England and Captain Taylor) and Kanhoji Angre. Both these missions were staged from Bombay.

The Royal Navy's Commodore Thomas Mathew led this mission (1722–1724) in the north Arabian Sea. This region had become infested with European pirates because of the successful suppression of piracy by the British in the Bahamas, the establishment of law and order on these islands, and an unconditional pardon to pirates who gave themselves up by 1 July 1719. It was those pirates who did not give up their wayward ways and simply shifted operations to the Arabian Sea who were responsible for the increased incidences of piracy. Many built enclaves in Madagascar and the French colony of Mauritius (Biddulp n.d.).

The four Royal Navy warships, which were supported by the Bombay Marine, carried out two major operations. One swept through the north Arabian Sea via the Persian Gulf and the Red Sea to the Isle of Madagascar. In spite of the high hopes riding on this first mission, it was an abject failure. The European pirates were always one step ahead of the fleet, despite the sweeping patrol of the seas.

The second was the unsuccessful assault on the impregnable sea fortress of Gheria (Vijaydurg in Sindhudurg district, Maharashtra). Everything from bad planning, unfavourable winds and bickering with the Portuguese viceroy turned it into an abortive attempt.

It was only in 1756 that the Company succeeded in defeating the Angres, but not during Kanhoji's lifetime. After his death in 1729, Kanhoji was succeeded by his two sons Sambhaji (headquartered at Gheria) and Manaji (headquartered at Kolaba). Of the two Sambhaji was the more feared of the two sons of Kanhoji. He even demanded an annual *hafta* (protection money) of Rs. two lakhs from the Company to leave their ships untouched.

It was due to a rift between the Peshwa and his Angre admiral, that the Peshwa Nanasaheb joined his Maratha forces with Admiral Charles Watson to bring the recalcitrant Tulaji Angre (who succeeded Sambhaji), in line. Watson's fleet had anchored at Bombay en route on a mission to fight the French in the Deccan, a fall-out of the ongoing Anglo-French war in Europe.[12] Maratha forces joined the English to storm the mighty fortress of Gheria, the headquarters of Tulaji, on 13 February 1756.

Yet again the Company used internal rivalries and insecurities between regional powers to secure its position on the subcontinent.

For the Maratha confederacy, it was a red-letter day in their history: the subjugation of the Konkan Coast was the first step in the decimation of the Company's most formidable foe – the Marathas – at sea and on land.

By 1818, Maratha power in the Deccan had been subdued with the decisive defeat of Peshwa Baji Rao II. The fallout was positive for Bombay: for the first time, the city had its own hinterland with most of the Deccan coming under its sway. The cotton growing tracts of Maratha country, as well as the route to the opium growing regions of the native kingdoms in the Malwa plateau opened to Bombay's trade. Both commodities were instrumental to the city's flourishing trade with China, which is detailed in the next chapter.

The end of piracy in Kutch and the Persian Gulf

At the same time that piracy was being crushed along the Konkan Coast, repeated attempts were made to subdue piracy in the indented coastline of Kutch and Kathiawar. This had been attempted in 1807, 1809 and 1812. But it was a final assault in 1819 by the Royal Navy and the Bombay Marine on the pirates of Kathiawar at Dwarka and at Beyt (termed in colonial accounts as 'robber's isle') that was decisive.

Most pirates in this region, like the European privateers, enjoyed the patronage of their rulers. It was because of the pirate's allegiance to his ruler that political treaties with these Kutch kingdoms were used by the Company to eradicate piracy and expand its influence. Naval anti-piracy missions combined with diplomacy, finally eradicated Kutch piracy.

The same approach was used to subdue piracy in the Persian Gulf.

For Bombay's merchants, the Bussorah (Basra)-Baghdad trade and the Persian port of Bushire (Bandar Bushehr) were the important nodal hubs for sea borne trade in this region. The most persistent pirates in the Gulf were the Qawasim tribal confederacy (today's Emirates of Sharjah and Ras Al Khaima). In spite of numerous expeditions against the Qawasim, the English found it hard to enforce peace terms as the Qawasim kept returning to piracy.

Just as in the case of the Angres, here too the English took the help of the rival dynasty of the Busaidis of Muscat and Oman, who were then under the British sphere of influence. Ironically, the British anti-piracy effort against the Qawasim was supported by another pirate – Rahma bin Jabr – the Qawasim's arch enemy and competitor of the Jalama tribe of Qurain (present-day Kuwait) (Bose 2009).

An earlier anti-piracy expedition of 1809, launched from Bombay, had inflicted just a temporary setback on the Qawasim. Therefore, the largest joint expedition by the Royal Navy and the Bombay Marine set out from Bombay in November 1819. The Qawasim put up a fierce fight against this formidable force, but were finally subdued when their citadel at Ras al Khayyam (Ras al Khaima) was overrun on 9 December.

Controlling the Qawasim Arab chiefs after that was an uphill task. It required a permanently stationed police force, and seven more treaties had to be signed after the first 'General Treaty of Peace' not just with the Qawasim but also with other regional sheikhs. In the view of British colonial chroniclers, the treaties finally transformed the 'pirates coast' (the stretch in the Persian Gulf from Oman to the peninsula of Qatar) to the more manageable 'Trucial Coast' (Treaty Coast).

Although the Trucial Coast was never part of Bombay Presidency like Aden and Sind, it's foreign and monetary policy was administered from Bombay. As Chapter 5 explains, because of Bombay city's centrality to trade and finance in the Arabian Sea region, it managed the fiscal and monetary policies of the Trucial States well into the 20th century.

Undergirding all these major successes of the Bombay Marine and the Royal Navy during the 18th and 19th centuries was the critical and abundant information that the hydrographic surveys – carried out by the Bombay Marine – of the main shipping routes yielded. There is a rough correlation between the Bombay Marine's hydrographic surveys and the naval wars, piracy missions and the expanding influence of this city and its presidency.

Hydrographic surveys and naval battles

Some important linkages that the Marine established was through the near-simultaneous exploration of the shipping routes of the north Indian Ocean and the Bay of Bengal by its marine (hydrographic) surveys. Over the next 100 years, these surveyed littoral regions were either annexed or brought under the Company's sphere of influence.

The earliest survey of the north Indian Ocean by the Company was done in 1703, by John and Samuel Thornton. The Europeans brought scientific mapping of the trade routes through the use of instruments to navigation in the Indian Ocean, where for centuries navigators had only relied on star navigation and visual landmarks as aids.

This enhanced intelligence of the seas was indispensable to the Company (later the British Crown) during patrols, wars and bad weather. For example, during the monsoon of 1756, Commodore James of the Bombay Marine crossed the turbulent seas with a fleet from Bombay to Calcutta. This established that communication between the east and west coasts was possible even during the monsoon season. This feat could not have been achieved without a thorough mapping by the Bombay Marine of the coastal sea routes, and it underscored the value of an effective marine hydrographic service. This timely reinforcement of 500 men that Commodore James's Fleet brought with it to Fort William (in Calcutta) later helped Vice Admiral Watson and then Colonel Robert Clive to capture Chandernagore, the French enclave (upriver from Calcutta) in March 1757, a major blow to French power on the subcontinent.

The first marine survey (1772) by the Bombay Marine covered the Makran coast in Sindh (now Sind in Pakistan), Kathiawar (in present-day Gujarat), portions off the Coast of the Arabian Peninsula and the Persian Gulf. This first expedition led to the founding of the Marine Survey of India (1785) in Bombay, by Captain (Sir) Charles Malcolm. Captain Malcolm was the first officer of the Royal Navy to head the Bombay Marine, which usually employed its own officers and men. His enthusiasm for mapping the oceans also led to the first survey of the Red Sea, an ancient shipping route that later became the high road between the west and the east with the opening of the Suez Canal in 1869 (Edwardes Vol. 2 1909).

It was the partial survey of the Persian Gulf in 1772 (First Survey) which was followed by some important actions in this region: the extermination of piracy in the Gulf by 1819 (described earlier), followed by the siege of Mocha on the Arabian Peninsula in 1820, and the action against the Beni-ibn-Ali Arabs of Iraq in 1821. The latter expedition secured the Bombay–Basra–Baghdad trade route. This was followed by a detailed survey of the Persian Gulf in 1821.

Another important correlation between hydrographic surveys and territorial inroads made by Great Britain was the survey of the East Coast of Africa, as far south as Zanzibar in 1811. This region was subjected not just to intensive patrolling by the Royal Navy and Bombay Marine for anti-piracy but also for anti-slavery. The biggest slave marts here were Zanzibar and Mozambique. In the early half of the 19th century, Zanzibar was ruled by the Omani sultan and Mozambique by the Portuguese. By the last quarter of the 19th century, Omani-ruled Zanzibar, Pemba and the Mrima Coast were all within the British sphere of influence.

The seas a bridgehead for territorial expansion

The most important contribution of the Marine was to the expansion of Bombay Presidency (1708–1936). This resulted in the overarching influence of Bombay city on everything across these annexed regions – from trade to monetary policy, justice, administration, and law and order.

By 1803, the Marine had secured the immediate vicinity of the seven islands, including Salsette island, the harbour islands, Surat (from the Nawab in 1800) and Bankot (Fort Victoria) in south Konkan. Another major phase of expansion of the Presidency in which the Bombay Marine played an important role was the Anglo-Mysore Wars against the sultans of Mysore Haider Ali and his son Tipu – detailed in Chapter 2.

By 1853, Bombay Presidency had taken shape: in the northwest, it incorporated Sindh (Sind); the peninsula of Kathiawar (part of Gujarat today); the districts of Gujarat (partly taken from the Mughals and the Marathas); and with the exception of the native kingdoms of Kutch, Portuguese enclaves, like Daman and Diu, the Sidi enclaves (like Janjira) and a few coastal kingdoms, it continued in one sweep right down the coast to the Portuguese capital city of Goa. Additionally, Aden had been annexed in 1839 and was ruled from Bombay.[13]

On the global stage, the Bombay Marine – a private navy of a chartered company – fought alongside the Royal Navy. During the Napoleonic Wars with France, the Marine was involved in the capture of Pondicherry, Trincomalee, Jafnapatnam and Colombo. It also played an active role in the final moments of the Egyptian campaign against the remnants of Napoleon Bonaparte's army in 1801, and in the capture of French Mauritius by the Royal Navy (1810).

These expansions catapulted Bombay city and its port to become the focal point and conduit for all trade from the Red Sea, the East African coast, Persian Gulf, the Makran coast, the Gulfs of Cutch and Cambay (now Kutch and Khambhat), and the Canara, Malabar and Travancore coasts. This was its immediate vicinity – the Arabian Sea littoral. The city also became a major transshipment port for trade with ports in the Bay of Bengal, the Strait Settlements (Malacca, Penang and Singapore), South-east Asia, China and Japan. The opening of the Suez Canal in 1869 further enhanced its commercial importance, whilst also making its Bombay Presidency ports of Aden and Karachi major transportation and shipping hubs.

Though the Bombay Marine played a strategic role in securing Bombay, its trade, its hinterland and overseas territories – through outright acquisition and/or gunboat diplomacy – it wasn't the only reason for making Bombay a confluence for commerce and culture. As Chapter 2 – 'The port and the city' – explores, a virtuous cycle of prosperity began with the development of its port, the city's first large-scale manufacturing – ship-building – and the trade wars it fought to secure teakwood supplies for this, and the China trade, which made its merchant communities prosperous.

Notes

1 This was the formal title of the EEIC from 1600 to 1708. When the Old Company merged with the New East India Company (a company that also acquired a charter later from the Crown), the merged entity was renamed the *United Company of Merchants Trading to the East Indies* (1708–1873).
2 Other riverine ports in the vicinity of Bombay islands were Thana (today's Thane), Callian (Kalyan), Portuguese Bassein (Vasai) and Chaul (Revdanda).
3 The Malabar Coast is part of the State of Kerala.
4 Marco Polo was on his return voyage home after visiting the kingdom of the legendary Kublai Khan (the first Mongol ruler of China).
5 The Royal Indian Navy remained headquartered in the city till 1944. It shifted to New Delhi for purposes of better coordination with the army and air force during the Second World War. Since then, independent India's naval headquarters have remained in New Delhi, although its main blue water fleet – Western Fleet – has continued to be headquartered in the city.
6 Three Presidencies – Bombay, Madras and Bengal – were formed after the amalgamation of the Old and New East India Companies in 1702/1708.

The first act of the reorganised Company was to form three presidencies in order to bring their scattered territories on the subcontinent into a formal administrative setup. Each Presidency was independent of each other, initially, till 1773, when Bengal Presidency took precedence over the other two.

7 A renewed Charter in 1773 appointed a Governor General (the first was Warren Hastings) in Bengal to supervise all the Company's Indian possessions.

8 Although the term 'admiral' is used for both the Sidi of Janjira and Kanhoji Angre, the fact remains that the terrain, the distance from the Mughal and the Maratha capital, and the fluid political situation in the Deccan both during the time of Shivaji and after his death, meant that the Sidi and Angre were largely acting on their own accord. Angre had been appointed *Sarkhel* (Admiral) by the Peshwa in 1698. He broke away from the Peshwa in 1704.

9 The seven islands were handed over to Sir Humphrey Cooke, representative of King Charles II and the first deputy governor of Bombay, at the Quinta.

10 After Kanhoji Angre's death his kingdom went first to his son Sekhoji. Unfortunately, Sekhoji died within a year and a fight broke out between his sons Sambhaji and Manaji. A truce was brokered by the Maratha Peshwa and North Konkan (headquarters was the Kolaba Fortress at Alibaug) went to Manaji, and South Konkan (headquarters was the fortress of Gheria) went to Sambhaji. Manaji captured Karanja and Elephanta, while Sambhaji maintained his foothold in Kenery or Kandheri.

11 One who traded without the licence, or outside the service of a Company (e.g. the English East India Company, which had a Royal Charter giving it a monopoly to all trade east of the Cape of Good Hope thereby forbidding other English merchants to trade in the same region).

12 This fleet had on board Col. Robert Clive and English regiments, which led the landward attack on Gheria. This same fleet proceeded to Fort David (Cuddalore) and then in November to Fort William (Calcutta). It fought in the Battle of Plassey (1757) that brought Bengal under English rule.

13 Included in Bombay Presidency were the territories of several kingdoms that had lapsed to the Company, as the rulers did not have legitimate legal heirs. Some – like the Kingdom of Baroda – had taken British Protection.

Bibliography

Biddulp. n.d. *The Pirates of Malabar*. Accessed May 7, 2017. http://www.colombia. edu/itc/mealac/prichett/00generallinks/biddulp/08chapter.html.

Bose, Sugato. 2009. *A Hundred Horizons: The Indian Ocean In The Age of Global Empire*. Cambridge, MA:Harvard University Press.

Das Gupta, Ashin. 1994. *Indian Merchants and the Decline of Surat*. Reprint 1994. New Delhi: Manohar Publications.

Downing, Clement. 1737. *A Compendious History of the Indian Wars with an Account of the Rise, Progress, Strenght, and Forces of Angria the Pyrate*. London: T.Cooper.

Edwardes, S.M. 1909. *The Gazetteer of Bombay City and Island Volume 1.* Reprint 1978. Bombay: Gazeteer department Government of Maharashtra.

English East India Company. n.d. "Surat Factory Records." Maharashtra State Archives.

Indian Navy. n.d. *Indiannavy.nic.in.* Accessed July 1, 2016. http://indiannavy.nic.in/content/ins-angre.

Lentin, Sifra. 2013. *Gateway House: Indian Council on Global Relations.* November 25. Accessed July 14, 2017. http://www.gatewayhouse.in/26.11-lest-we-forget.

Malgaonkar, Manohar. 1981. *The Sea Hawk: Life and Battles of Kanhoji Angrey.* New Delhi: Vision Books/Orient Paperbacks.

Maloni, Ruby. 1992. *European Merchant Capital and the Indian Economy: Surat Factory Records 1630–1668.* New Delhi: Manohar Publications.

Ray, Himanshu Prabha. 1994. "Kanheri: The Archaeology of an Early Buddhist Pilgrimage Centre in Western India." *World Archaeology* 26 (1): 39.

2 The port and the city

The early modern history of Bombay islands[1] is deeply connected to the seas. As detailed in the previous chapter, the Company leveraged the islands geo-strategic location to expand its trade and influence in the Indian Ocean region. So, it is fitting that this chapter covers key sea-related facets of the city – the city's first large scale manufacturing – ship-building; the two trade wars to secure teakwood supplies for its ship-building, railways and exports, and its seaborne China trade. The latter was largely responsible for the creation of intermediate capital for its merchant community, which they invested in building Bombay's textile mill industry, modern banking, reclamation and insurance companies all of which began in the 19th century.

Bombay's integration into global shipping and trading routes took off only by the mid-17th century and by 1870, it had become a global hub for trade and finance. During these 200 years, it became the capital city of Bombay Presidency (1707–1936), and an axis of political and financial power for the British in India (especially across West Asia, East Africa and among the islands of the Arabian Sea). Its centrality was exemplified by the reach of its presidency, whose territories included overseas Aden (now a part of Yemen) and Sindh (now in Pakistan). Bombay's influence accelerated because of its location, its well-developed and connected port, ship-building facilities and the fact that it was the headquarters of a powerful naval force. The coalescing of these key developments triggered a virtuous cycle of economic prosperity in the city.

Ship-building: Bombay's first large-scale manufacturing

The city's earliest large-scale industry is the Bombay dockyards. Ship-building as we know it today was first established on the islands by the Parsi master builder,[2] Lowjee Nusserwanjee Wadia, who immigrated

DOI: 10.4324/9781003182894-2

to Bombay from Surat in 1736 (Wadia 1983). The ship-builders of Surat were famous, many of them Parsis. And Wadia's work as shipwright was noticed by George Dudley, the master attendant (marine) in Bombay, who travelled to Surat to oversee the construction of a Company ship 'The Queen'. Wadia and a team of 12 artificers (carpenters) were persuaded by the Company's Bombay Council to shift to this city and establish the Company's ship-building yard.

It would be a simplification to state that Bombay had no ship repairing and building facilities before the arrival of Lowjee. The earliest reference, dated 23 April 1672, is to an English ship's carpenter being sent to Bombay by the Surat Council, and after this date, there are numerous references to ship-building facilities, shipwrights and specialised carpenters on the islands.

Initially, Wadia and his team remained under the supervision of Robert Baldry, a master carpenter, till 1740, during the construction of their first seven ships, including the first namesake of the city – the Bombay grab. Bombay's shipyards, however, did not acquire the fame that they did as a ship-building facility till the arrival of Lowjee and his team. During Lowjee's lifetime (1710–1774), he built 57 ships, many for the Company's service in Bombay, and also for the Company's Bengal Pilot Service, its fort and factory at Madras, and for private merchants (Wadia 1983).

His contribution to building armed grabs, schooners, brigantines, ketches and sloops for the EEIC, and country ships (large merchant ships) for trade in Bombay is inestimable. The armed ships were mostly used for convoying merchant ships trading with the Persian Gulf and the Red Sea ports. The Company itself had outposts and residents in the Gulf regions, like at Bussorah (Basra), during the 18th century, to facilitate trade (Wadia 1983). The Surat Factory Records (1622–1708 and 1718–1804), housed in the Maharashtra State Archives (Mumbai), have numerous entries of armed convoys accompanying merchant fleets between Bombay and Surat. These ships also play an important role in the early anti-piracy missions (see chapter one) launched from Bombay, which secured these routes for trade.

How Wadia ships linked Bombay to the world

The fame of the Wadia-built teakwood ships spread after the British Admiralty began ordering warships built in Bombay. At first, during the latter half of the 18th century, the Admiralty began acquiring already-built ships. Its earliest acquisition was the 'Swallow' (built in 1777) and renamed the 'Silly' by the Royal Navy.

The reason for the Admiralty looking east for its warship acquisitions was the severe shortage of oak in England during the 18th century. The intermittent wars with France (notably the Seven Year War between 1754–1763, and the Napoleonic Wars of 1792–1815) and Holland (the Fourth Anglo-Dutch War of 1780–1784) made it difficult to acquire this raw material on the Continent. Oak timber was largely sourced from the Baltic states, which since 1500 had provided timber, tar, pitch, hemp, flax and copper, for ship-building in Europe.

By the 19th century, warships were also built in British colonies like Calcutta, Pegu (today's Bago port located on the River Pegu in southern Myanmar) and the Prince of Wales Island (today's Penang Island, located in the Strait of Malacca).

Altogether, Bombay Dockyards built 16 'ships of the line' (warships) out of 39 ships acquired or built to order for the Royal Navy. These were among the approximately 365 ships built by the seven Wadia master builders (shipwrights) till 1932 (Wadia 1983; Koffend 1979). Building ships for the Admiralty meant that draft drawings, copper bolts, sheathing and other special stores were shipped from England to Bombay to meet the exacting standards of the Royal Navy. Some of these Admiralty ships constructed in Bombay went on to make history, many of them constructed by Lowjee's grandson – Jamsetjee Bomanjee Wadia (master builder from 1792–1821). Wadia-built ships were legendary for their sturdy construction and the quality of their teak hulls and masts.

The Royal Navy warship the 'Cornwallis' (the fifth Royal Navy ship by this name), built and launched in Bombay dockyards in 1813, became famous as the Treaty of Nanking (29 August 1842) between the British and the Chinese was signed onboard this ship. This treaty brought an end the First Opium War (1839–1842) and led to the opening of five more treaty ports in addition to Canton (Guangzhou), and it confirmed the ceding of Hong Kong Island on lease to Great Britain. Effectively, it opened the Chinese mainland to foreign trade. It was Bombay's China trade – dominated by cotton (later cotton yarn) and opium – that many economic historians attribute as the reason not just for great wealth among the city's merchants during the 19th century, but for creating capital for its textile mill industry (RN).

Probably the most well-known Wadia-built ship is the HMS Minden, the first ship-of-the-line[3] to be built outside England. This 74-gun ship with a tonnage of 1,721.5 was built in 1810 by Jamsetjee Bomanjee Wadia in Bombay shipyards. The 'Minden' is famous because the American national anthem *The Star-Spangled Banner* was composed by American poet Francis Scott Key while he was held captive on board and was watching the bombardment of Fort McHenry in Baltimore, Maryland (on 15 September 1814), by the Royal Navy fleet.

Another historic Wadia ship was the HMS Salsette – the first ship built to order for the Admiralty and the first teakwood ship in the Royal Navy, and launched in 1805. So sturdy was this ship that it withstood, undamaged, nine ice-locked weeks in the north Baltic Sea, while every other accompanying ship was either crushed or floundered. The Salsette was returning to England while convoying a fleet of 12 merchant ships in the winter of 1808–1809. It survived the harsh winter in an ice-locked Baltic was probably due to the excellent timber used in its hull, a fact highlighted in person by the ship's first lieutenant, when thanking Jamsetjee Bomanjee Wadia for saving his life and all those aboard this ship, a few years later (Wadia 1983). Another highlight of the career of the 'Salsette' was its participation in the Baltic Wars, both the Gunboat War (1807–1814), a naval conflict with Denmark-Norway and the Anglo-Russian War of 1807–1812.

But the oldest surviving Wadia sailing ship still afloat is the teakwood warship HMS Trincomalee, built in Bombay by the Wadia master builders and launched on 12 October 1817. After an exciting career as a naval ship and patrol ship (against slavery in the Atlantic Ocean), it was finally retired in 1986 – after active service of 169 years. This ship is still seaworthy and the only remaining Malabar teak warship from the Wadia era that was made in the Bombay dockyards. It remains on view at the National Museum of the Royal Navy in Hartlepool, UK.

Trade follows the flag: the battle for teakwood

By the early 18th century, Bombay was fully integrated into the global world of Indian Ocean trade. It must be noted that this world was not a creation of European colonisation that began with Vasco Da Gama in 1498, but of a vibrant trading system that has existed since the 8th century CE[4] (Goiten and Friedman Mordecai 2008; Alden n.d.). What the Portuguese achieved by their discovery of the Cape route to the East Indies in the late 15th century was to connect the Atlantic maritime world to the Indian Ocean one via the Cape of Good Hope – a direct sea route.

Bombay's late entry into this network coincided with intense European rivalry in the Indian Ocean region, which was often a spill over of those on the Continent. Bombay's fortunes – more specifically – were greatly impacted by the Anglo-Mysore Wars in the Deccan.[5] Haider Ali, the sultan of Mysore, and his son, Tipu Sultan, had French advisors in court as well as French army officers, soldiers and arms. The three Anglo-Mysore Wars were in reality trade wars between the French-backed Kingdom of Mysore against the English and their allies (the Marathas, the Nizam of Hyderabad and the Kingdom of Travancore).

The first war began with Haider Ali's invasion of the Malabar in 1766. This invasion directly impacted the trade of the EEIC in Bombay, as the Malabar region was a rich source of pepper, spices, sandalwood, rice and teakwood. The Mysore kingdom itself had extensive forests of teakwood, which were out of reach not just for the Company but also for private British traders and interlopers.[6] More importantly, by the early 18th century, a triangular trade between India, China and England was well-established. Bombay had begun exporting short-staple Deccan cotton to China by 1730. A valuable part of this bilateral trade was teakwood.

Instead of paying for Chinese tea, silk and porcelain, in specie and silver, Bombay became the êntreport (transhipment port) on the subcontinent's west coast for the supply of cotton, spices, pepper and teakwood. Teakwood imports into Bombay from the Konkan and the Malabar forests met not just the needs of Bombay's shipyards but also the demand in the Chinese market. The city was supplying goods that China needed and Britain did not produce (Nightingale 2008).

The Treaty of Seringapatam (1792), signed after the defeat of Tipu Sultan in the Third Anglo-Mysore war, resulted in the ceding of the coastal districts of Malabar, Salem, Bellary and Anantapur to the Company. With this, the Company also captured a monopoly in teak logging in the Mysore territories. The province of Canara (Kanara) and Malabar were initially incorporated into Bombay Presidency, but after the Partition Treaty of Mysore (1799), both were incorporated into Madras Presidency. Bombay retained its logging rights; however, Canara was later transferred to it in 1861 (Maclean 1875). Another war in which Bombay's ship-yards, railways and merchants had high stakes, especially for securing a good supply of teakwood, was the Third Anglo-Burmese War. Here a listed Bombay company was the direct trigger for a war whose sole aim was to create a monopoly in teakwood logging in the pristine forest of the Upper Burmese kingdom (Figure 2.1).

The Bombay Burmah Trading Corporation and the Third Anglo-Burmese War

By a twist of fate, The Bombay Burmah Trading Corporation Ltd. is the holding company of Bombay Dyeing & Manufacturing Co. Ltd. This makes it part of the Wadia group of companies; its chairman,

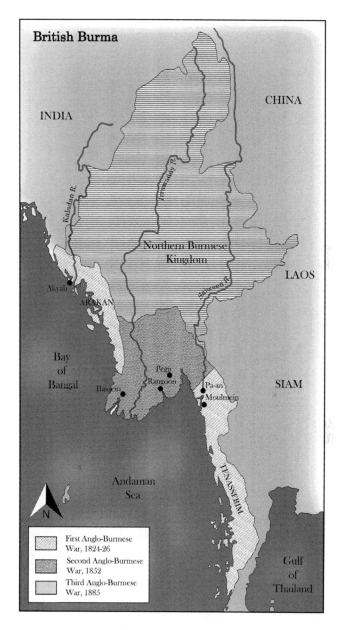

Figure 2.1 Map of British Burma showing regions annexed from 1824 to 1885.
Source: From the collection of Sifra Lentin.

Nusli Wadia, is a direct descendant of the famed Wadia ship-builders family, known for their long association with teak timber.

The original trading corporation made its fortune in Burma teak. The company, which today has coffee and tea estates, and other manufacturing interests, was mainly a teak lumbering and trading entity in Burma in the late 19th and early 20th centuries. Its merchant, William Wallace, was among the first loggers in the then pristine rainforests of Upper Burma (now a part of Myanmar). This Bombay company was also the trigger for the third and final Anglo-Burmese war (1885–1886) against Upper Burma. It was a war that gave Great Britain a monopoly over Burmese resources, particularly its much-valued teakwood forests.

The Bombay Burmah Trading Corporation Ltd. was originally founded as Frith & Co (Bombay) in 1837, a partnership firm between a Bombay-based merchant Framji Nusservanji Patel and a Scotsman from Edinburg, J.G. Frith. The partnership firm largely dealt in Manchester piece goods (cloth); it was also an agent for the British Government of Ceylon for sourcing a variety of goods from the sub-continent and England. It changed its name to Wallace & Co. when the Scottish Wallace family became a partner.

The trading interests of this firm changed drastically when the oldest of the six Wallace brothers, William, visited Burma to oversee the supply of 1,500 tons of teakwood that had been contracted from a firm from Moulmein, Lower Burma. This supply was destined for Bombay and for work on the railways in India. William witnessed in the (by then British) southern Burmese provinces of Arakan, Pegu and Tenasserim in 1855, which had harbours on the rivers Irrawaddy, Sittang and Salween, respectively, a brisk trade in teak. These territories were already part of British ruled southern Burma after the conclusion of the First Anglo-Burmese War (1824–1826) and the signing of the Treaty of Yandabo (24 February 1826) between the Burmese and English.

An indication of the scale of business in teak, which was by then needed to build the railways in India, provide for the shipyards, as well as supply exports to England and China, was a report of 1886 by Sir Dietrich Brandis, the first British conservator of Burma's forests. He states that between the years 1857 and 1864, approximately 85,000 tons of teakwood was exported every year. And from 1883 to 1884, the annual average export was 275,000 tons (Pointon 1963).

As the Lower Burma forests slowly depleted because of excessive logging by various companies that bought teak concessions (permissions), logging companies began looking north to the Upper Burmese kingdom. One of the earliest to make an inroad in acquiring logging concessions from King Mindon, and later from his son King Theebaw, was William Wallace.

These concessions were viewed as risky in Bombay by the partners of Wallace & Company. The Upper Burmese kingdom was totalitarian (which meant that contracts could be rescinded on a whim), and the still simmering friction with British-ruled southern Burma made large investments in North Burmese teak concessions financially risky. To minimise this risk, the partnership firm of Wallace & Co. floated a new company – The Bombay Burmah Trading Corporation – this way, it could monetise William's investments in Burma. This company was incorporated on 4 September 1863, and William Wallace's risky Burma ventures were acquired by it in 1864.

The time coincided with the share market boom of 1863–1865 in Bombay, which was fuelled by money pouring into the city due to the demand for Indian cotton. The American Civil War (1861–1865) had led to an embargo on exports of American cotton from the southern American states, which starved England's textile mills of raw cotton. Bombay's hinterland of present-day south Gujarat and former Maratha territories (by then under Bombay Presidency), including the cotton growing tracts of present-day Karnataka, made the city the transhipment port for the export of the coarser short staple Deccan cotton to England.

But in just 20 years after its incorporation, the Bombay Burmah Trading Corporation found itself mired in an international 'incident' at the Tinsel Court of King Theebaw at Mandalay (Upper Burma). It was fined Rs. 22 lakhs by the *Hutlaw* (Imperial Council), which believed the company had logged more than it had paid for. This contentious claim between the *Hutlaw* and a British Indian company came at an opportune time. Sir Winston Churchill, in his biography of Sir Randolph Churchill, his father and secretary of state for India (June 1885-January 1886), referred to the *Hutlaw's* contentious claim as the 'lucky incident' that gave Great Britain the excuse to invade Upper Burma in the Third and final Anglo-Burmese War (1885–1886) (Pointon 1963). Incidentally, King Theebaw, Queen Supalayat and their family were exiled in Ratnagiri, a coastal district south of Bombay islands, then part of its Presidency. In a moving tribute to the exiled Burmese royal family in her book *The King In Exile: The Fall Of The Royal Family Of Burma,* author Sudha Shah describes how the exiled King Theebaw spent his last days observing through his telescope ships moving past the coast of Ratnagiri, evidently to and from Bombay. Little did the exiled King realise that the port city of Bombay was by then the axis for security, commerce and culture in the western Indian Ocean, and the reason for his downfall.

Burma teak was an important part of the valuable Bombay–China trade, whose better-known goods were cotton and Malwa opium. It was the China trade – often used as a euphemism for the highly lucrative but illegal (in China) opium trade – that not only brought great wealth to Bombay and its merchants but also ruined many a Bombay family fortune in the aftermath of the First Opium War (1839–1842) (Figure 2.2).[7]

The seaborne China trade

The export of raw cotton from Bombay port to China began sometime in 1730. It followed on the heels of a famine in the south eastern provinces of China, which resulted in a Chinese imperial edict prohibiting the cultivation of cotton in the region. This necessitated cotton imports into this region through the port of Canton (Guangzhou), the only Chinese port then open to foreigners.

The timing was fortuitous, as almost parallel to this was the increasing popularity of Chinese tea in England. The demand for Chinese tea expanded exponentially soon after the passing of the Pitt's Commutation Act (1784) that lowered the tax on tea imports from 112% to 12% ad valorem in order to curb the smuggling of tea from the Continent into England.

To meet this demand for Chinese tea, as well as pay for it without draining the English treasury, the EEIC, which then had a monopoly in both the India and China trades, tried to pay for tea with other goods. But English-manufactured goods were not in demand in China, so Indian cotton stepped in to supply a much needed Chinese demand. However, after these initial trading decades, by the turn of the 19th century, it was Indian opium that was increasingly sent to bridge the adverse balance of trade that Great Britain had with China. And this was in spite of the clandestine nature of the opium trade. Opium was a banned substance in China since 1729.

The reversal of the flow of silver to China is evident in the numbers: between 1752 and 1800 a net of $105 million (silver), which was approximately £26.25 million, went to China. However, between 1808 to 1856, $384 million flowed into England's coffers. The tipping point was the enormous Indian opium imports absorbed by China (Lowell 2011).

This also coincides with the years when the export of Malwa opium from Daman, Goa and subsequently from Karachi expanded enormously. The export of opium from Bombay Port was banned in

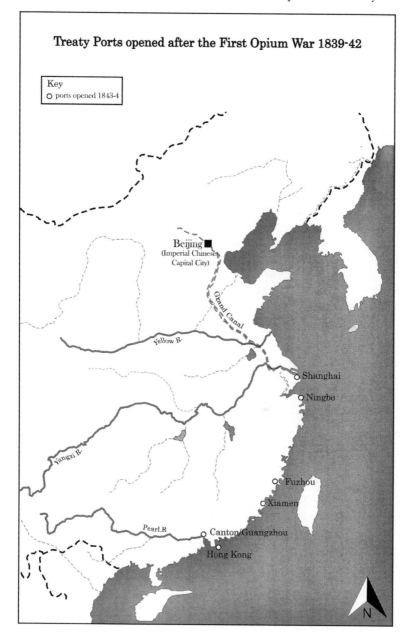

Figure 2.2 Map of Treaty Ports opened after Anglo-Chinese War (1839–1842).
Source: From the collection of Sifra Lentin.

1805, because Malwa opium breached the EEIC's monopoly of the Patna (Bengal) opium trade from Calcutta. Opium cultivation and processing in Bengal Presidency was monopolised by the Company, unlike opium exports from the west coast that was grown in native kingdoms of the Malwa plateau region, like the Kingdoms of Baroda and Indore. Moreover, Malwa opium was cheaper and appealed more to the Chinese peasant than Bengal opium. The export of opium from Bombay Port only restarted in 1830 after the company realised that neither had they succeeded in stopping the exports of Malwa opium from the Subcontinent's west coast but were in fact losing an enormous amount of revenue (Claude 2009).

The opium trade from Bombay was facilitated largely by the European Agency Houses, like Bruce Fawcett & Co., Forbes Smith & Co. and Alexander Adamson, who did so for local and European merchants alike on the basis of a consignment system, just as they did for cotton. This opened up this lucrative trade even to small investors, although the system was inherently weighted against them. The Agency Houses before the advent of the British overseas banks and foreign banks were an important source of silver for the EEIC's resident in Canton, and they facilitated the remittance of funds (alongside the Company) to the subcontinent and London for their clients (Dwijendra 2004).

The trade from the subcontinent's west coast was a highly democratised and cosmopolitan venture, unlike Calcutta, as the hinterland growing opium and the routes through which the readied commodity transited through to reach Karachi – then under the Baluchi Talpur Amirs – and Portuguese Daman, Diu and Goa ports between the years 1805 and 1830 and after that British Bombay, were controlled by native kingdoms. The big merchants who controlled this trade, however, were based in British Bombay and Ahmedabad, and Portuguese Goa. These merchants in turn were supported by an indigenous network of *gomastas* (agents), rulers and officials from the native kingdoms where opium was grown or where it transited through overland, and Marwari *sahukars* (moneylenders), who were the point of contact with the peasants who grew the poppy plant.

Sir Jamsetjee Jeejeebhoy – the first Indian to be awarded a baronetcy and Bombay's biggest *sethia*[8] in the early half of the 19th century – expanded his China trade exponentially after 1818,[9] when he brought in business associates from outside his family and community circle (Palsetia 2015). Diverse networks were necessary to survive in the China trade. Some of Jamsetjee Jeejeebhoy & Co.'s associates at various points were the Jain merchant Motichund Amichund, the

Konkani Muslim Mahomed Ali Rogay and the Goan Catholic Roger de Faria. His agent in Canton was the Agency House of Jardine Matheson & Co., originally named Magniac & Co., whose partner William Jardine was a good friend of Jeejeebhoy.[10] Jamsetjee Jeejeebhoy & Co. and Jardine Matheson & Co. had a long-running business relationship in the China trade, with the latter handling all Jeejeebhoy's consignments and goods on the China end.

What drove these discursive partnerships and associations was the nature of the China trade itself – high risk, high return – especially *before* the First Opium War (1839–1842). After this first Anglo-Chinese war, the first-ever conflict China had with a western power, the nature of the trade changed with just a few big merchant houses like Sassoon and Tata from Bombay riding the second wave. The entry barrier for smaller merchants became prohibitively high.

The war had a terrible fallout on Bombay's China traders after the signing of the Treaty of Nanking (August 1842). The conclusion of the war in Great Britain's favour actually resulted in many Bombay fortunes being lost in its aftermath. Britain was slow in distributing the £21 million in reparations it received from Imperial China. This reparation was paid largely for the smuggled opium consignments destroyed by the Imperial Commissioner Lin Xexu on the banks of the Pearl River. Of the 20,000 opium chests surrendered by merchants under the jurisdiction of the British Superintendent of Trade – Charles Elliot – 7,000 chests belonged to Indian merchants. Of these, more than 1,000 belonged to a single Bombay merchant – Dadabhoy Rustomjee – a prominent China trader belonging to the Banaji family of Bombay (Thampi and Saksena 2009).

It is the appeals for reparations by desperate Bombay merchants as late as the 1860s that reveals the names of merchants whose consignments were destroyed by Commissioner Xexu as belonging to multiple trading communities in Bombay. The first list of 163 names consisted of one-third Parsis, with the rest being Jains, Marwaris and other Hindus. Though there are no Muslim names in this petition, a notification of 2 January 1864 by the Hong Kong government mentions 14 Ismaili (Khoja) merchants out of 28 compensated for their opium surrendered in 1839.

Post this war, most traders found it difficult to acquire good bills of exchange to repatriate funds home because in addition to competing with American and European merchants for bills, in 1833, the EEIC's monopoly of the China trade ended thereby opening the door to numerous private British traders into the China trade. Just 20 years earlier, the Company's monopoly on the India trade too had ended.

Moreover, as most Bombay merchants operated on short-term, high-interest capital this trade became financially unsustainable for them. The shortage of good bills even impelled Jamsetjee Jeejeebhoy to undertake the Canton-London-Bombay sector himself rather than through intermediaries – one instance being when Jeejeebhoy's ship the *Earl of Balcarras* carried goods to London from Canton in 1841 (Siddiqi 1982). The voyage was a dismal failure with the ship being inexplicably delayed in London's docks. This voyage alone cost him £5,000 instead of the estimated £2,000, underscoring how impractical it was to send country ships (meant for bulky cargo like cotton) to London – a route monopolised by British shipping interests.

Adding to the merchants' woes was not just the delay in receiving compensation but receiving a fraction of what was due to them. In spite of these inherent inequities in the colonial trading system, Bombay's trade with China was set to expand.

China and the making of Bombay's cotton mill industry

One of the most significant outcomes of the Bombay–China linkages, according to many Indian historians, is that the China trade in cotton and opium aided capital accumulation in the city (Thampi and Saksena 2009; Amar 2006). This eventually transformed Bombay from a site of mercantile activities to a centre of industrialisation. Most of Bombay's China merchants were knowledgeable about the workings of foreign trade (particularly with China), as well as about the cotton-growing hinterlands of Gujarat and central India. It was inevitable that they would take the next step into manufacturing cotton yarn and cloth.

The Parsi merchant Cowasjee Nanabhoy Davar set up the first cotton textile mill at Tardeo, Bombay, in 1851; this was followed by the Oriental Spinning & Weaving Company, founded by Maneckjee Nusserwanjee Petit in 1855. A little over ten years later in 1865, Bombay's merchants had set up ten mills of 25,000 spindles and 3,400 looms, that consumed 40,000 bales of cotton annually (Koh 1966). By the turn of the 20th century, the biggest mill owners in Bombay were the Petits (Sir Dinshaw Petit, son of Maneckjee), the Elias David (E.D.) Sassoon branch (headed by David Sassoon's grandson Sir Jacob) and the Ismaili Sir Currimbhoy Ebrahim. Also, by this time, the cotton mill industry was almost wholly concentrated in western India. It had grown up in and around the cities of Bombay and Ahmedabad. Bombay was the larger centre but by the beginning of the 20th century, Ahmedabad grew at a faster rate (Bagchi 2007). Jamsetjee Nusservanji Tata (the founder of the Tata Group) transitioned to manufacturing when he bought a disused oil mill in Chinchpokli (central Bombay) that he converted into his first textile mill – Alexandra Mills. This was followed by the setting up of the Empress Mills in the cotton growing region of Nagpur (which was the first to use the ring spindles which revolutionised in its time the manufacturing of cotton yarn), and then again, the Swadeshi Mills in Bombay. [11]

What is notable about the mill owners Sassoon (both branches – David Sassoon & Co. and E.D. Sassoon & Co.), Ebrahim and Tata, is that they all were deeply engaged in the China trade. Tata at one point even tried to breach the Peninsular & Oriental Steam Navigation Company-led dominance on the freight trade to the Far East by starting his own shipping line – Tata Line – in collaboration with the Japanese shipping line Nippon Yusen Kaisha (NYK) in 1894. His spirited attempt lasted a year, although NYK got a foothold into this busy route.

However, Bombay's cotton mill industry was not immediately successful. It faced sharp competition from the Lancashire and Manchester mills in the yarn and cotton piece goods markets of China, Japan, Africa and even in India. Moreover, Indian cotton was of a coarse, short staple, and was spun into yarn that could only be woven into coarser mill-made or handloom cloth, which did not sell well in Britain.

What supported the nascent mill industry in these early years was the enormous Chinese demand after 1870. The coarse Indian yarn was in great demand by the Chinese handloom industry. This explains the preference in the early years for establishing spinning mills rather than weaving mills in Bombay. However, the boom years of 1901–1902 to 1905–1906 for Chinese exports did not last. The exports of cotton twist and yarn sharply declined after peaking at 298.5 million lbs (1905–1906) and continuously declined to 152.3 million lbs and 198.9 million lbs in 1911 and 1914 (Bagchi 2007).

The competition in the early 20th century came from the indigenous Chinese and Japanese cotton mill industries. As early as 1893, Bombay's mill-owners were debating Chinese and Japanese competition in the yarn segment. Sir Dinshaw Eduljee Wacha, a prominent Bombay China-trade merchant and one of the founders of the Indian Merchants Chamber at Churchgate, observed: 'Chinese inertia is great. But it is also the national characteristic that once the inertia is removed, it moves with the velocity of an avalanche'.

But the tougher competition in this period came from Japan. From before the First World War and more so during the inter-war years, Japanese yarn and cloth was not only superior to Indian products, it was also cheaper because of greater labour productivity and superior technology. Japanese mills sourced their raw cotton directly from Bombay's cotton hinterland. At first, their two big suppliers were Tata & Sons (opened its branch in Kobe in 1891) and Sassoon & Sons (who opened branches in Kobe and Yokohoma), both Bombay-headquartered business groups.

In 1892, Indian raw cotton comprised 50% of total Japanese raw cotton imports. And during the inter-war years of 1922–1923, two Japanese companies (Tomen and Nichimen) were directly buying cotton from Bombay's hinterland to the extent that they handled 30% of all India raw cotton exports, not just to Japan but also China and Europe.

Although the cotton mills in Bombay had to adapt to deal with this competition by targeting the home market – they did this by diversifying in a big way to weaving, dyeing and printing cloth rather than largely spinning yarn. This transition was greatly helped by the Indian nationalist movement, particularly the Swadeshi Movement of 1905.

But the Indian cotton mill industry's enormous influence on government resulted in a differential tariff structure for British imports and other countries' (mainly Japan) yarn and piece goods imports – a strategy that backfired badly. By June 1932, duty was raised to 75% ad valorem with a minimum specific duty on plain grey goods of 6¾ annas per lb on all non-British imports. Japan reacted by boycotting Indian raw cotton, of which it had been the largest buyer. This friction caused by high Indian tariff on Japanese yarn and textiles was resolved only in 1934, when India and Japan signed the 'Indo-Japanese Trade Protocol'.

Today, Japan is not a major textiles manufacturer, but China dominates the entire value chain in production as well as exports. China is the largest exporter in the world of yarn, fabric, apparel and made-ups. India today has a significant share in yarn and fabrics, but dominates in raw cotton fibre as it did in the past. It accounts for 26% of world production, which makes it the second-largest producer of raw cotton in the world).[12]

Today, the smoke stacks that once dominated the Bombay skyline no longer exist, and, after a long decline of the city's textile industry since the 1970s–1980, only a few standing mills here speak of a once thriving textile-manufacturing hub which was largely brought about by the city's thriving China trade.

Notes

1 The seven islands of Bombay were: Colaba & Old Woman's Islands, Bombay, Varel (Worli), Parel, Mahim, Mazagaon, and Syva (Sion).
2 The term 'master builder' is used to describe the head of the shipbuilding department in Bombay, and remained in use till the department was abolished.

3 'Ship-of-the-line' is a reference only to historic warships constructed during the 17th century to the mid-19th century. The name is derived from the common naval manoeuvre from this period, in which two columns of opposing warships would face each other. Often, the weight of the broadside (right) guns on board would face the enemy ships.

4 The Indian Ocean trade routes gained ascendancy in the 8th century over the ancient land routes. The monsoon wind system, so important for ship-borne trade in this region, was said to be discovered by Hippalus, a Greek navigator and merchant, in the 1st century.

5 During the mid-18th century, the Anglo-French wars led to several naval battles between the two powers off the coast of Madras and Pondicherry. The EEIC had a factory at Fort St. George, Madras, and the French had an enclave close by at Pondicherry. Bombay too had several red alerts during this time, especially when a French naval ship sailed past the city.

6 Interlopers were British traders who had arrived on the subcontinent without the permission of the EEIC, which enjoyed a monopoly on trade east of the Cape of Good Hope as per its Royal Charter. Private British traders were those who were trading with the permission of the Company.

7 The First Opium War was the first war ever between China and a European power. The Treaty of Nanking (August 1842) that marked the end of this war is regarded in China today as the first of the 'humiliation' treaties. Imperial China fought three opium wars with the European powers.

8 'Sethia' is a term used when referring to a wealthy and influential native merchant. Jeejeebhoy made his fortune in the China trade and was also invested in a big way into real estate in the city, for which he received rental income.

9 Jamsetjee was in business with his uncle. It was only after the death of his uncle that his firm Jamsetjee Jeejeebhoy & Co. first entered into a part-nership with the Jain merchant Motichund Amichund and the Konkani Muslim Mahomed Ali Rogay. A little later the Catholic Goan Roger de Faria also joined as a business associate. This varied group contrasted sharply to the earlier family-run business, as each brought in their own networks and contacts. One example of this was de Faria, who used his influence with Portuguese authorities to allow Jamsetjee and his associates to ship cotton and opium from Daman at a time when the export of opium from Bombay was banned by the Bombay government.

10 Dr William Jardine and Jeejeebhoy had struck up a friendship during their imprisonment – both were captured when their ship headed for Canton was captured by the French during the Napoleonic Wars.

11 In 1886, Jamsetjee N. Tata established the Swadeshi Mills after re-furbishing the defunct Dharamsi Mills in Kurla, Bombay. Swadeshi Mills was started by him for weaving cloth of finer counts then only manu-factured by English mills.

12 The Cotton Corporation of India Ltd., (Accessed 11 September 2021) India's share in the world.cotcorp.org.in/national_cotton < http://cotcorp.gov.in/shares.aspx> (Kelkar 2015).

Bibliography

Alden, Oreck. n.d. *Modern Jewish History: The Cairo Genizah.* http://www. jewishvirtuallibrary.org/jsource/History/Genizah.html.

Amar, Farooqui. 2006. *Opium City: The making of Early Victorian Bombay.* New Delhi: Three Essays Collective.

Bagchi, Amiya Kumar. 2007. *The Evolution of the State Bank of India: The Roots 1806–1876.* New Delhi: Penguin India.

Claude, Markovits. 2009. "The Political Economy of Opium Smuggling in Early 19th C India: Leakage or Resistance?" *Modren Asian Studies* 43 (1): 89–111.

Dwijendra, Tripathi. 2004. *The Oxford History Of Indian Business.* New Delhi: Oxford University Press.

Goiten, S.D., Friedman Mordecai, A. 2008. *India Traders of the Middle Ages: Documents from the Cairo Geniza 'India Book' Part 1 & 2.* Leiden: Brill N.V.

Kelkar, S. S., interview by Sifra Lentin. 2015. *Cotton Growing Hinterland of Bombay* (March).

Koffend, John B. 1979. *Bombay Dyeing: The First Hundred Years 1879–1979.* Bombay: The Perennial Press.

Koh, Sung-jae. 1966. *Stages of Industrial Development in Asia: A Comparative History of the Cotton Industry in Japan, India, China and Korea.* Philadelphia: University of Philadelphia Press.

Lowell, Julia. 2011. *The Opium War: Drugs, Dreams and the Making of China.* London: Picador.

Maclean, James Mackenzie. 1875. *Guide to Bombay.* Bombay: Bombay Gazette Steam Press.

Nightingale, Pamela. Reprint 2008. *Trade And Empire In Western India 1784–1806.* New York: Cambridge University Press.

Palsetia, Jesse. 2015. *Jamsetjee Jeejeebhoy of Bombay: Partnership And Public Culture In Empire.* New Delhi: Oxford University Press.

Pointon, A.C. 1963. *The Bombay Burmah Trading Corporation Limited 1863-1963.* London: Wallace Brothers & Co.Holdings, Ltd.

RN, William Loney. n.d. http://www.pdavis.nl/ShowShip.php?id=61.

Siddiqi, Asiya. 1982. "The Business World Of Jamsetjee Jeejeebhoy." *Indian Economic and Social History Review* 301–324. Vol. XIX, Nos. 3 & 4.

Thampi, Madhavi, Shalini Saksena. 2009. *China and the Making of Bombay.* Mumbai: The K.R. Cama Oriental Institute.

Wadia, Ruttonjee Ardeshir. Reprint 1983. *The Bombay Dockyards And The Wadia Master Builders.* Bombay: Neville N. Wadia for Messrs. Nowrosjee Wadia & Sons (Pvt) Ltd.

3 Migrants in the city and their overseas networks

One approach to understanding Bombay's overseas spheres of influence is to trace the history of its multicultural migrant trading communities and their overseas networks. Some of these diasporas were created *before* Bombay the trading city existed BUT were transposed here when these communities made the city their spiritual and community headquarters.

The city became attractive to these internal migrants from the 18th century onwards because of its relative security, trade, commercial and connectivity advantages on the west coast – both overseas and inland. This spurred Indian trading communities to shift to the city. The EEIC government actively encouraged these enterprising communities, largely those concentrated in Surat and its vicinity during the 17th and 18th centuries, to Bombay, by offering religious freedom and tax breaks. Large influxes occurred at inflexion points like droughts, famines, epidemics and political upheavals in their home cities, towns or villages.

Not only did these communities – Bhatia, Jain, Marwari, Bohra, Khoja, Memon, Parsi and later Partition refugees, like Sindhi and Sikh – build entire community ecosystems in the city (places of worship, community halls, schools, colleges, hospitals, orphanages, housing) but also individuals who succeeded enormously contributed to the building of the city itself. The sheer scale of merchant philanthropy in Bombay makes it unique among Indian cities, especially when compared to the British Indian capital cities of Calcutta (1772–1911) and later New Delhi. Merchants donated to the building of the city's key institutions like hospitals, universities, research and educational; infrastructure like the Mahim Causeway (donated by Lady Avabai Jeejeebhoy, wife of Bombay's merchant prince Jamsetjee Jeejeebhoy), and even landmarks – like the ceremonial arch of Gateway of India at Apollo Bunder.

Far more pertinent are the overseas community networks they spawned but nurtured from the city. Though these networks were

DOI: 10.4324/9781003182894-3

driven by business and sustained by profits, a diaspora presence increased when manpower from the community pool, brides and even entrepreneurs actively circulated between the city and its diasporic nodes. The more profitable and promising a region was, the more resources – goods, credit and manpower – would be invested in it.

What is important is that 200 years later these networks still exist between the city and West Asia, East Africa and Hong Kong, while connections between former strongholds like mainland China and Japan are diminished in contrast to their robust historic presence.

It is the western arc of the Subcontinent's coasting trade with the Arabian Sea littoral comprising the Persian Gulf (Oman, Iran), West Asia and East Africa that is home to the earliest presence of trading communities from India's west coast. One of the oldest, strongest and culturally richest networks still remains the Bombay–Oman–East Africa overseas connections (Figure 3.1).

Slaves, ivory and cloves: the East Africa trade

Oman takes centre stage in the links between Bombay and East Africa as an historic axis of trade between the two regions. Its centrality began with Omani hegemony since the 17th century over most of the island states off the East African coast and its control of the mainland Mrima coast[1] opposite Zanzibar Island (the Omani capital in Africa sometime from 1832–1840), which facilitated trade not just with Bombay but also with Britain, America, France, the German-speaking Hanseatic states and later Germany.

The Omani Arabs then under the leadership of the founder of the Ya'arubi dynasty Imam Sultan ibn Saif rose in revolt and threw the Portuguese out of Muscat in 1650. Soon after, in 1652, the Sultan sent a small fleet to raid the islands of Pate and Zanzibar. This began the Omani intervention in East Africa (see Table 3.1). Pertinently, the Omanis were the first maritime power[2] to break the 16th-century Portuguese stranglehold over the Indian Ocean trade routes, partly reclaiming Arab control over trade and shipping in this region.

By 1658, the Omanis had acquired Zanzibar, and in 1698, they wrested Fort Jesus in Mombasa from the Portuguese. Omani dominion, from the mid-18th century, now under the current Busaidi dynasty, continued over this region (with the exception of Portuguese-ruled Mozambique and its surroundings) till the late 19th century before they yielded to Great Britain. However, their control over this region was more akin to a soft hegemony to facilitate trade rather than territorial acquisitions with clearly defined borders (Roland and Mathew 1963).

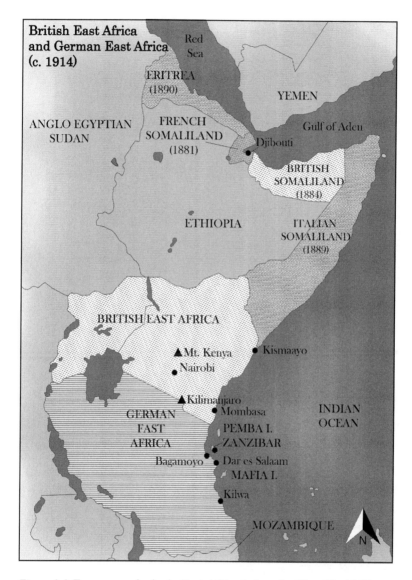

Figure 3.1 European colonies in East Africa before the First World War.

Source: From the collection of Sifra Lentin.

Table 3.1 Portuguese-controlled ports in the Persian Gulf and East Africa which came under Omani rule

Port/region	Years of Portuguese rule/ tributary state	Year of Omani acquisition
Muscat	1507–1552 and 1588–1650	1650
Hormuz	1507–1622	1798–1868 (leased from the Persians)
Mombasa (East Africa)	1593–1698 and 1728–1729	1698-1728;1729-1887 (between 9 February 1824 to 25 July 1826 it was briefly a British Protectorate before it was restored to Omani rule in 1826). Relinquished in 1887 to IBEAC.
Islands of Zanzibar and Pemba	1503 or 1504–1698	1698

Broadly, the Omani-controlled choke points in the Arabian Sea were Zanzibar, Mombasa and Muscat, all watering stations and important trade marts *before* the opening of the Suez Canal in 1869. This hegemony extended to the port of Gwadar (now in Pakistan), controlled by them till 1958, which gave them victualling home ports for their *dhows* on the route to the subcontinent (Kaplan 2011).

Making the most of Omani control in the maritime sphere by early 17th century, a considerable community of Hindu merchants (largely Bhatia from Rajasthan and Gujarat) settled in Muscat, Hormuz, Aden and Zanzibar. They were joined by Muslim Khoja, Bohra and Memon communities from the subcontinent's west coast. It was from here that a few ventured to trade with Lamu, Mombasa, Bagamoyo, Kilwa, Lindi, Zanzibar and Pemba, in the wake of these ports and regions coming under Omani control or political influence (see Table 3.1).

Portuguese-controlled ports in the Persian Gulf and East Africa that later came under Omani rule

In these early years, Indian merchants traded in Muscat dates, Arabian and Persian horses, gold and slaves from Sofala (on the East African coast), ivory from East Africa, Indian piece goods (cotton cloth), food grains from India and Chinese porcelain and silks. It was largely an intra-Asian (coastal) trade between the ports of the Red Sea, Persian Gulf and the merchants' bases at Mundra, Mandvi and Cambay (Khambhat) in the region of present-day Gujarat.

Much before this 17th-century influx of Kutchi-speaking Hindu Bhatia and Muslim Memon, and Bohra and Khoja (the latter two are largely Shia communities) from Sindh, Kutch and Saurashtra, were the Gujarati-speaking Jain community who appear to be the earliest to establish itself in the Portuguese colonies of East Africa, namely the ports of Mombasa and Kilwa and Mozambique. Although the popular impression is that Jains are an austere community, their history in this region underscores that their success was in fact due to their adaptability to different milieus and mores, even endowing mosques in the medieval port cities of Gujarat, like Cambay and Bhadreshwar, for their fellow Arab and African traders[3] (Mehta, Gujarati Business Communities in East African Diaspora 2001).

The migratory movement of Indians from Oman to the East African littoral region, especially its islands of Zanzibar and Pemba, was triggered after Omani Sultan Sayyid Said decided to shift his capital to Zanzibar from Oman between the years 1832 and 1840. This move was initiated on the advice of his trusted advisor, the Bhatia merchant Sewjee Topan (1764–1836). Many Indian traders were co-opted into the Sultan's mission to have unrivalled control over the East African slave trade. Zanzibar and the Portuguese colony of Mozambique were both major slave marts in this region during the 18th and most part of the 19th centuries.

The East African slave trade was more a collaborative venture between Indian traders and local Swahili-speaking merchants, who were a mix of Arab and African stock. It was the Swahili merchants who ventured into the interiors of the African mainland in search of slaves. Slaves then formed the bulk of the labour working in plantation economies like French Mauritius and Reunion islands. They were also used to transport ivory to the coast, as beasts of burden were vulnerable to attack by the deadly tsetse fly. It was the trading part – slaves and ivory – where Indian merchants were active in.

Indian traders as mentioned earlier were also involved in the lucrative export of gold, while imports included Indian cloth, spices, food grains, Chinese porcelain and silk. It is in this arch of the *dhow* trade – stretched from the East African coast and further east to Aden, Muscat and Hormuz, Gwadar, Sindh, before reaching the west coast of India and Bombay by the late 18th century – that the early seaborne circulations of manpower occurred.

Omani Bhatia: pioneers in linking Oman to India's west coast

The Kutchi-speaking Hindu Bhatia merchant community from the princely kingdoms of Kutch and Kathiawar (like the Halai Bhatia) were among the first Gujarati trading communities to settle in large numbers in West Asia and East Africa. The famous Bhatia merchant Sewjee Topan encouraged other traders from his homeland, like the Bohra hardware merchant Budhabhoy Noormuhammed, to send his son Jivanjee (father of Karimjee, founder of the 196-year-old Karimjee Jivanjee Group, Tanzania) to Zanzibar in 1823. To date this family – now eight generations old in East Africa – and headquartered in Dar-es-Salaam (before that Zanzibar) since 1943 are the oldest franchisees for Toyota in Africa (Oonk 2009). This family till the Second World War had an office in Bombay's Bruce Street (renamed Sir Homi Mody Street) to facilitate their business with the city.[4]

The recruitment of manpower from the family and community pool to run and expand overseas businesses is the common narrative thread for Indian merchant settlements, with the exception of Japan where local staff was preferred. But for the Omani Bhatia the partnership with their Arab host was sweetened by religious tolerance. This understanding can be traced back to the 17th century, when the Arab rulers of Muscat, orthodox Ibadhi Sunni Muslims, allowed Gujarati Hindus to construct a Pushtimargi Vaishnav (Shreenathji Nathdwara or Krishna) temple in Muscat.

This was reiterated recently when the late Sultan Qaboos bin Sa'id wanted to extend his palace grounds. He offered a valuable location to the resident Omani Indians to build a new temple in place of two old ones. Muscat now has two temples: a new Shreenathji temple that houses two idols, and an old Shiva temple (Khimji 2015). This religious tolerance and partnership between Arab and Hindu traders historically stems from the important concerns of trade. Arabs had dominated the Indian Ocean trade since the advent of Islam in the 7th century AD. However, it was the Gujarati-speaking merchants' acumen for numbers that made them indispensable to the Arabs.

According to Jaisinh Mariwala, the patriarch of the Mumbai-based Bhatia Mariwala family,[5] the Bhatias have tremendous goodwill in Oman. Some established Bhatia families, like the Khimji Ramdas family, the Dharamsis and the Naranji Hirjee family, have been there for generations and are all citizens of Oman – Omani citizenship being hard to acquire. All these prominent Omani families historically have had a strong business presence in Bombay, but are known only in business and community circles, as they choose to remain low profile.

The importance of these Omani citizens of Indian origin who are non-Muslim is underscored by the privilege they have been given – they are *not* subject to the Islamic Sharia Law in Oman. This emphasises how much the Sultan values their presence in Omani society.

In fact, the late Sultan Qaboos bin Sa'id's cousin is married to the great-grandson of Khimji Ramdas, Ajitsinh Gokaldas Khimji.

An insight into how these old linkages work: many big Indian and foreign companies now have a presence in Oman through a resident Indian Omani. This includes the Shapoorji Pallonji conglomerate, who have built the Sultan's palace in Muscat, Larsen & Toubro, the Tata Group and Dabur. With the exception of Dabur, all of them are headquartered at Bombay, demonstrating the continuing centrality of Bombay in spheres from infrastructure, construction, finance, banking and the traditional trading.

The Hindu Bhatia have maintained a distinct religious presence in Oman, while the old Memon and Khoja families have intermarried with the local Arabs because of a common religion. Families who returned from Zanzibar to settle in Oman mostly speak Swahili in addition to Arabic. However, the vital link among the Indian Khoja and the Bhatia communities is their language Kutchi, although the Khojas speak a variant of Kutchi called *Khojki*.

It was the ancestors of the old, established Omani Indian community that joined the entourage of Sultan Sayyid Said and his advisor Sewjee Topan to Zanzibar during the years 1832–1840. Although the Sultan signed anti-slavery treaties with the British, beginning as early as 1803, the slave trade from Zanzibar did not stop till the last treaty of 1873 was signed between Sultan Barghash and the British envoy, Bartle Frere, the much beloved former governor of Bombay. The demise of the Zanzibar slave trade resulted in the decline of this Island's mercantile economy. What made business there still attractive was the triangular ivory trade, with Bombay port as its pivot.

The triangular trade of Zanzibar–Bombay–London

Since the late 18th, 19th and early 20th centuries, Bombay was the axis of trade between Zanzibar and London. In retrospect, it appears absurd that goods from Zanzibar intended for London had to take the circuitous route via Bombay even after the Suez Canal opened. But there were good reasons for Bombay becoming a nodal port for this trade. The main one being Indian traders in Zanzibar and their compatriots who anchored the trade from Bombay.

By 1811, Indian merchants were well-settled in Zanzibar, and by 1819, numbered 214. Though numerically small and only men at this point, in 1811, about 50% of imports into Zanzibar were *Surats* (cotton cloth) traded by Indians. What was exported by them were slaves, ivory, gum copal (used in making varnish) and – after the

signing of the anti-slavery treaties (earliest 1803 and the last 1873) –
abundant quantities of clove. Indian capital in Zanzibar was then di-
verted to clove plantations where slave labour was used.

However, what was the most valuable part of this triangular trade
was ivory, traditionally imported in great quantities by Indian princely
kingdoms to make bangles. India was the biggest market for ivory, its
consumption waned with the subjugation and impoverishment of the
princely kingdoms due to British hegemony. Where once 80% of the
ivory imported at Surat and Bombay was consumed within India,
this began stagnating by the early 19th century. Strangely, the quantity
imported into Bombay actually increased substantially. While the local
markets absorbed an annual average of Rs. 283,000 (1800–1810) and
Rs. 225,000 (1810–1820), the average annual imports during these two
decades were Rs. 375,000 and Rs. 437,000, respectively (Sheriff 2002).
This indicated a growing export trade from Bombay port.

One of the reasons why this triangular trade through Bombay
flourished was the preference by British and American traders to deal
with Indian merchants in Zanzibar, especially after 1841, when a British
Consulate was established there. All commercial disputes between them
were first heard before the Consular Court, and appeals were heard in
the High Court in Bombay. Unfortunately, the imperatives of trade and
Zanzibar's economic decline put paid to this triangular trade.

North Sudanese and West African ivory soon toppled the dominance of East African ivory exported via Bombay (see Table 3.2). The
glut in clove production in Zanzibar, Pemba and on the Mrima Coast
brought down not just the price of this commodity but irretrievably
sank Indian capital invested in them.

Table 3.2 A comparison of the sources of ivory exported to London

Year	India/ Bombay	North African	East African (direct trade)	South African	West African	Total/ price per ton
1852	221	86	2	44	73	453/£685 per ton
1875	178	167	160	72	152	813/£950 per ton

- In tonnes
- Sheriff (2002)

Bombay: the axis for trade, community and enterprise

The late 17th and early 18th centuries were the years when the first wave of migrants – largely mercantile communities from the princely kingdoms of Kutch, Kathiawar and their ports of Mandvi, Porbandar, Diu, Cambay and the Mughal port of Surat began immigrating to Bombay. They were actively encouraged by the Company government but more often untenable conditions – droughts, oppressive taxes, political instability and insecurity – disrupted trade in their home ports and kingdoms and were the reasons that drove families to settle in this colonial city. Big native firms too opened branches in the city before shifting their headquarters here because of Bombay's growing commercial importance.

It is important to explore how community, financial and religious networks brought by internal migrants to Bombay, replenished their overseas diasporas with manpower, capital and religious leadership, thereby keeping them within the community fold. With the exception of the Parsis and a few well-to-do merchants who settled in the Fort, most early migrants resided in the native town, which was located north of and outside the walled city – Fort area – in South Bombay. Their original place of residence is still milestoned by their religious-community ecosystem that they built during the 19th century, and which serve the same function it once did.

The Bhatia community, like other Gujarati- and Kutchi-speaking communities (Jain, Patidar, Lohana, Bohra, Khoja and Memon) in the city, immigrated in large numbers in the late 18th and early 19th centuries. Many well-known families among them like the Mariwala and Seth Laxmidas Khimjee family (after whom the Laxmidas Khimjee cloth market is named) made their fortunes *after* settling in the city. The trajectory of the Mariwala family, which gets its name from *mari* (pepper), chronicles the opportunities and hardships that early pioneers faced when they migrated to Bombay.

The family came to Bombay in the 19th century, and eventually entered the trade in Malabar spices and coconut (which they still do). Jaisinh Mariwala's great grandfather arrived as a young boy of 13 years, who began life in the city by stitching bags that would carry goods transshipped from Bombay harbour. He says that the Bombay of the 18th and 19th centuries was a great entrêport, and ships had to be turned around quickly. For this, goods brought in had to be repackaged for export. The young Mariwala slept on unstitched bags at the ware-houses that run adjacent to the port and run north from the Indira (Alexandra) Docks at Ballard Pier. From here, began the family's lin-kages with the rest of the world.

Trading families like the Mariwala's used to then live in Mandvi, just north of Crawford Market. In fact, the family still retains its old office here. This precinct lies flush along the dockyards and is still home to large warehouses and *peedhis* (a traditional place of work where *Hundi* bankers and brokers, and traders operate from). Even today, business worth crores of rupees are transacted in the wholesale markets here.

Like most Bhatia families of the time, the Mariwala's also estab-lished a branch on the Malabar Coast, from where they sourced spices, copra (dried coconut kernel) and various Malabar products, and then networked through family and community to Oman and East Africa. It was from Oman and East Africa that date, *kharek* and, later, clove were imported by them into Bombay.

The Seth Laxmidas Khimjee family too arrived in the city penniless in 1843. According to Swami Anand, in his classic source book on the Bhatia community, *Kul Kathao (1966),* it was the high tariffs on the Bengal-Dhaka cloth – a most popular Indian import into England – combined with a fine of £50 on those who purchased this fabric that the export market for Indian handloom cloth was killed. This was a protectionist measure to support and popularise English mill-made cloth which was exported in large quantities to India. This marked an upturn in the fortunes of many Bhatia cloth traders who dealt in English mill-made cloth, like Jivraj Baloo, Kanji Chatur and Seth Laxmidas Khimjee, who became a leader of the Bhatia *Mahajan.*

Bombay's wholesale markets for cloth, food grains and spices were dominated by Bhatia traders from the mid-19th century to the Depression years (1929–1930) that followed the First World War (1914–1918) (Herdeck and Gita 1985) and were a main import source in the subcontinent for the Gulf and East Africa. This community, like the Parsis and Baghdadi Jews, also ventured into textile mills,[6] oil mills, ship-building (Hindustan Shipyards at Vishakhapatnam) and shipping (Scindia Steam Navigation Co. and Varun Shipping Co. Ltd.).

The Hindu Bhatia community's religious and community institu-tions are administered by a Bhatia Mahajan, with its current head-quarters in Bhatia Baug, Kalbadevi, very close to their oldest temple – Sri Dwarkadhish – also on main Kalbadevi Road. This precinct is also where they settled in large numbers because it is close to the many markets where they traded – and still do.

In contrast to the Bhatia, where a community council prevails, the Ismaili Khoja community exemplifies how the active intervention of their Imam – the Aga Khan – established the community's institutional linkages between their headquarters (in Bombay from 1848 to 1957) with East Africa, at first.

This institutional connection between Bombay and East Africa was in fact the first overseas outreach by the Aga Khan. It was a model that was emulated and developed over a period of a 100 years in other parts of the world, wherever a sizeable Aga Khan Khoja community was present. But this community superstructure – now known as the Aga Khan Development Network (AKDN)[7] – a not-for-profit umbrella global organisation that oversees religious, community and non-denominational institutions (schools, colleges, universities, hospitals and the like which are accessible to the host population) had its beginnings in Bombay.

There were two events that occurred in Bombay that profoundly shaped the future of what was to grow into a 15 million strong global community, with their largest concentration in the Subcontinent (India and Pakistan), the Gulf countries, Africa, Central Asia, Europe, the United States and Canada.

First, was the arrival of Hasan 'Ali Shah, the 46th Imam and the first Aga Khan (an honorific bestowed on him by the Persian emperor, Fath Ali Shah), who settled in Bombay city in 1848. He was the first Ismaili Imam to set foot in the Indian subcontinent. His arrival marked the beginning of the modern period in the community's history. Prior to the 1800s, the Ismaili Shia Imams were based in Persia[8] and had limited contact with the Ismaili communities that were scattered across Central Asia and Afghanistan – where they were concentrated along the Silk Road – the Middle East and South Asia. With the Imamate shifting from the province of Kirman (Iran) (IIS 2015) to Bombay, the Ismaili Imam came into full public view, his presence having an invigorating effect on local Khoja Ismailis and many distant communities from Central Asia, who sent missions to the city to meet him (Daftary 2011).

Second, the authority of the Ismaili Imam was challenged in three cases[9] that were adjudicated by the Bombay High Court, and together effectively legalised the hereditary temporal and spiritual power of the Aga Khan. But it was in the third and last case – Aga Khan Case (1866) – that the Ismaili Imam's authority over British Indian Ismailis was legally delineated – and resulted in a schism within the community, with a breakaway faction (the Ithna Asheris) being formed, which is an equally large Khoja community in the Subcontinent and Africa.

It was after this that the Aga Khan began consolidating his following by reforming their religious beliefs and practices, and setting up an institutional framework that would be administered according to a common constitution.

During the 19th century, the community was largely settled in the Dongri area, also close to the city's eastern foreshore of warehouses and dockyards. It is here that the city's oldest existing Ismaili Khoja *jamaatkhana* with its stately clock-tower – Darkhana – on Samuel Street, was built in 1923, replacing an older *jamaatkhana* (according to community lore) on the same spot. The former Aga Khan palace at Mazagaon, with it legendary stable of horses tended by Persian ostlers, is today the Prince Aly Khan Hospital, was once the focus of community affairs.

The Aga Khan's first official tour overseas was initiated in 1905 during H.E. Sir Sultan Mahomed Shah Aga Khan III's visit to Zanzibar and East Africa to connect with his congregations, some of whose male members had immigrated in the early 1820s much before Aga Khan I settled in Bombay. The community's first rule book, titled *The Rule Book of the Khoja Shia Imami Ismaili Council: Part 1&2* by Hussein Chapkhano, was instated for the local community by Aga Khan III in Zanzibar (Daftary 2011). It was here too that the first Supreme Council to regulate community life was set up.[10] Both the rule book and council governance are features of Ismaili community organisations worldwide. It was in Kisumu (Kenya) though, where the first *jamaatkhana* (community hall) in Africa was inaugurated the same year. Well-known Khoja merchant Seth Allidina Visram funded it. It is well-known that Visram encouraged not just young men from his community to seek their fortune in the then British Protectorate of East Africa but also those from other Gujarati and Kutchi communities.

The enterprising Dawoodi Bohra community, much like their neighbours in Kutch and Saurashtra – the Hindu Bhatia and the Aga Khan Khoja – settled in Muscat, Hormuz and the Omani dominions in East Africa *before* their migration to Bombay. Often, the Bohra trader chose to settle with his family overseas, unlike the Hindu merchant and his staff, who kept their families in their home town and villages.

Community lore says that the first wave of Bohra traders migrating to East Africa took place in the aftermath of a severe drought in Kathiawar. The 43rd Syedna (the Bohra spiritual and temporal leader) called 12,000 of his followers from this parched region to Surat, his then headquarters, and provided food, work and lodgings for all of them. His only condition was that they learn certain vocational skills, and that in return he would pay them their earnings for work done only when it was time for them to leave Surat. When he disbursed lump sum payments to them at the end of their stay, many from this group decided to use this capital to venture forth to trade in East Africa. Family histories, like that of the successful 200-year-old Karimjee Jivanjee family formerly headquartered in Zanzibar but in Dar-es-Salaam since 1943, also speak of intra-community networks being instrumental in wooing young men to seek their fortune overseas.

It was from Zanzibar, which once hosted the largest overseas Dawoodi Bohra settlement, that inroads were made into the East African mainland in the second half of the 19th century. This was done in the wake of European colonisation of Tanganyika[11] (German), and Kenya and Uganda (British). It was then that Bombay's connections with this mainland region, and with its British Indian subjects already resident there, became pivotal politically and administratively, because of its close proximity to East Africa.[12] This triggered a second and larger wave of settlers from the city and its Presidency.

Parallel to this second wave of migration was a sizeable settlement of this community in 19th-century Bombay. The city, because it was a nodal transshipment hub, acted as a springboard for trade and immigration for the Dawoodi Bohra to other Indian Ocean islands like Madagascar, Mayotte, Ceylon, South East Asia, as also to the Far East – mainland China, Hong Kong and Japan.

Referring to this growing Bombay presence, a community document of 1813 refers to the first Bohra Masjid, today known as Badri Masjid, within the Fort area of the city being endowed by a local merchant Chandabhai Seth or his heirs (Feeroz 2020), an indicator that a thriving community was already resident in the city. Another record from 1830 to 1831 states that there were 150–200 Bohra shops in the vicinity of their mosque on Bohra Bazaar Street – named after this enterprising community who owned most of the shops here. This street runs parallel to Dadabhoy Naoroji Road, where Badri Masjid stands. Badri Masjid, along with Saifee Manzil – the residence of the Dawoodi Bohra religious and temporal leader Syedna (or Dai) – on Malabar Hill, is the administrative headquarters of this community (Iftitah Bina al Masjid al Badri al Hani n.d.).

Notwithstanding this sizeable Bombay community, and the fact that the Syedna was officially acknowledged in 1772 by the English Company in Bombay as native nobility and also later nominated to the Bombay Presidency's legislative council,[13] Surat continued as the headquarters of the Dawoodi Bohra. In the meantime, an *Amil* or senior religious scholar was appointed early on by the *Dawat* or religious council, to look after community affairs in the city.

The Bombay community – largely traders and shopkeepers – prospered greatly from the growing economic importance of the city, which was *Urbs Prima In Indis* or the first city of India. Travelers' accounts over time tell of the community's thrift, colourful clothes, cheerful disposition and enterprise. A vivid example is how the import of kerosene oil into Bombay gave rise to a new industry, with the Bohra traders buying empty tins for about two annas each and fashioning them into lanterns, boxes, trunks, oil pots and other articles for sale (The Gazetteer of Bombay City And Island 1909).

The official transfer of the *Dawat* and the *Dai*'s residence to Bombay is milestoned by the Raudat Tahera mausoleum in Bhendi Bazaar, where the 51st *Dai* – Syedna Taher Saifuddin (d. 1965) – is buried, as is the 52nd *Dai*, his son Syedna Burhanuddin (d. 2014), indicative that they lived and worked in the city. Though the administrative headquarters shifted to Bombay, the cultural ecosystem of Surat as epitomised by its over 200-year-old *Sayfi Dar*, the foremost institute for higher Islamic studies, took decades to take root in Bombay. But today this loop is almost closed, with the *Aljamea-tus-Saifiyah* college, an institute for advanced Islamic Studies, being established in Mumbai, and the fact that 21st-century internet technology has made the *Dawat* in Mumbai accessible to its one million strong Dawoodi Bohra community abroad and in India.

It was on this foundation of an institutional community ecosystem and a strong presence of Gujarati and Kutchi-speaking traders in the wholesale markets of Bombay from the mid-19th century that business and diasporic networks between the city and British East Africa took off in the 1890s. This was also a time when Bombay's hinterland was secured. One outstanding example of this integration between the local and its overseas communities is exemplified by the Bombay and colonial Tanganyika–Kenya–Uganda network.

Mainland East Africa and Bombay

The old merchant community slowly began immigrating from Zanzibar [14] to the German colony of Tanganyika (today's mainland Tanzania) and the British East African colonies or what was to become the nations of Kenya and Uganda. A new wave of migrants from Bombay Presidency and the kingdoms of Kutch, Saurashtra (Kathiawar) and Gujarat began replenishing this old diaspora. This broadly occurred after the failure of the Imperial British East Africa Company (IBEAC) in 1895. The IBEAC was a public limited company founded on 18 April 1888 by Sir William Mackinnon, a Scottish expat merchant based in Calcutta. The company went bankrupt just years after Mackinnon's death in 1893. Mackinnon was also the founder of the shipping agency Mackinnon, Mackenzie & Company, and the then largest shipping line in the world, British India Steam Navigation Company (BISN), both of which, though head-quartered in Calcutta, had a strong presence in Bombay, which was a home port for its Haj shipping route and the Bombay–Karachi mail packet service.

BISN's ships and subsidiary shipping lines touched almost all ports from the Gulf, the Red Sea and the East African coast from Bombay (Aim25 n.d.). This shipping line in particular was famous for its cuisine prepared by the Goan cooks it employed in large numbers, from then Portuguese Goa.

When the British foreign office took over IBEAC in 1895–1896, the Kenya–Uganda railway line project took off. Known as the Uganda Railway, it was to run from Mombasa to Kisumu (on Lake Victoria). This was Mackinnon's most cherished plan, and surveys had already been completed, but he did not succeed in raising the funds.

The implementation of this massive railway project at a cost of £5 million attracted merchants like Seth Allidina Visram from Zanzibar to East Africa.

Bombay was the port of supply for most provisions for the labour recruited from the subcontinent to build the 582-mile-long railway line. The abolition of slavery by 1873 led to indentured Indian 'coolie' labour being recruited for this project and being shipped first from Karachi (Sind) and later from Bombay. The Uganda Railway was executed in five years (1898–1905) at a tremendous cost of human life and livelihoods. Of the 31,983 labourers, 6,454 were declared unfit for work, while 2,493 died during the construction of the railway line (Metcalf 2008).

In his autobiography *Tide of Fortune: A Family Tale*, the late Manubhai Madhvani of the Madhvani family of Uganda writes that this Railway was a golden opportunity for Seth Allidina Visram: "As each section of track was completed, he followed with commercial premises. He opened a shop at every large station along the 580 miles of railway; provided food, clothes and all necessities for the workers on the railways; set up a branch of his trading empire in Kampala in 1898, and then opened stores in Jinja, up along the Nile in southern Sudan, and also in Kenya and Congo.[15] (Madhvani and Foden 2009).

Seth Visram was a big *dukkawala* (shopkeeper), a term that was and is commonly used by local Africans when referring to Indians. In fact, most big families – Karimjee Jivanjee, the Madhvani family of Uganda, and even the Mehta's from Kenya–Uganda, all began their businesses as shopkeepers and small traders. Visram's first chain of stores stocked goods of the highest quality, and catered to Indian and colonial officials. His trade also introduced local Africans to dealing in currency rather than barter. The Indian rupee was introduced as a monetary unit of exchange in East Africa through big and small Indian traders and shopkeepers, thereby resulting in its popular use (Bhanuben and Reynell n.d.; Madhvani and Foden 2009; N. K. Mehta 1987).

Visram's connections to Bombay were multi-pronged. He was in the traditional trade of cotton piece goods and food grains, but soon began specialising in the triangular ivory trade, where he earned the moniker 'King of Ivory', he entered into agriculture, notably growing cotton (Asians 2011). Many Indian merchants in Kenya and Uganda forayed into growing cotton and setting up cotton ginneries because of their connections with the Bombay cotton mill industry and commodities markets. Madhvani points out, 'In 1919, Indians were buying 50% of Uganda's cotton crop and exporting it to Bombay's textile mills' (Madhvani and Foden 2009).

Another Ugandan family, the Mehta's, were also suppliers of Ugandan cotton to Bombay's mills. The pioneer of this family, Nanji Kalidas Mehta, writes about his first Bombay consignment, 'Purchasing cotton on a big scale, I sent 12,000 bales to the textile mills of Sheth Mathuradas Gokuldas and sold some of the remaining bales elsewhere' (N. K. Mehta 1987). Today, the Mehta Group has its corporate headquarters in Mumbai, with businesses spanning not just Uganda but also the United States and Canada (Group n.d.).

Seth Visram was not just a mentor to new immigrants to East Africa but also sponsored the immigration of many young men from the Ismaili Khoja community to British East Africa. Specifically, in 1905 the Aga Khan III whilst on his first visit to East Africa encouraged Visram to expand the presence of the community here in light of the abundant opportunities (Madhvani and Foden 2009).

Besides the sourcing of manpower by Indian merchants and shopkeepers from their home towns and villages, a still ongoing process in the 21st century (of particular value are Indian teachers and accountants), were those who were recruited to man the Uganda Railway line. The British sourced *coolies,* surveyors and clerks; tracks, sleepers and coaches; training manuals; and later staff to man the line, from Bombay, and Karachi, which was part of Bombay Presidency. The city's Great Indian Peninsula Railways (GIPR) and Bombay, Baroda & Central Railways (BB&CI) were there to replicate[16] (Metcalf 2008).

Although most of the coolie labour used to build the Uganda Railway returned home to the subcontinent, the young men who were wooed by the opportunities to set up businesses of their own in the region after earning their spurs under an experienced merchant, like Visram (he guided the founders of the Madhvani and Mehta business empires), went on to form the backbone of the plantation economies in this region. Large merchant families, who diversified into tea, coffee and sugarcane plantations, succeeded because of the business and family connections they retained with Bombay and in present-day Gujarat, which is still a source of their staff. They also initiated basic industries in this region after the independent nations of Kenya, Uganda and Tanzania (includes Zanzibar) were formed in the 1960s.

Civil war followed closely on the heels of independence in East Africa, the worst part of it being the brutal regime of General Idi Amin in the 1970s, which consisted of a mix of internecine tribal warfare (300,000 Ugandans died) and the acquisition of properties and businesses of affluent East African Indians. Most Indians fled to the UK, United States and Canada (Madhvani and Foden 2009; Bhanuben and Reynell n.d.). Political and economic stability returned to this region only in the 1990s. African leaders wooed back the big Indian plantation owners and industrialists with the offer of restitution of their businesses. This began a virtuous cycle of skilled Indian workers from the subcontinent again moving to East Africa – just as they had done in the past.

Partition's Sindhi refugees and their global networks

The widest global diaspora network ever that the city of Bombay inherited post-independence was that of the Hindu Sindhi refugee community. A majority of those who arrived in the city by sea from Karachi in 1947–1948 were settled in what was then known as the Kalyan Camp (military barracks used during the Second World War and converted into dormitory-style shelters for the refugees). Renamed Ulhasnagar township (or the new township of Ulhasnagar by Governor General C. Rajagopalachari on 8 August 1949), it is today part of Mumbai Metropolitan Region. Where once most residents of Ulhasnagar were Sindhis in this township of 13 square kilometres, today less than half of its population of eight lakh people are Sindhis.

The most attractive aspect of the then Kalyan Camp for the refugees who settled there was its proximity to Bombay even if it had no roads, water taps, flour mills, electricity or sanitation facilities (Hardas 2017). Other camps, like the one in Pune, to which refugees arriving at Bombay port were also sent, were considered too far away for the city's business and employment opportunities by the intrepid entrepreneurial Sindhis.

Many young Sindhi boys in those early days began life hawking knick-knacks, trinkets, and eatables made in Ulhasnagar, on trains running between Ambarnath and V.T. Stations (now Chhatrapati Shivaji Terminus). Much before Chinese goods came to be manu-factured at cheap rates, the Sindhis at Ulhasnagar were making just about anything at less than half the market price. Although, these goods were pejoratively referred to as 'Made in USA' (lit. Ulhasnagar Sindhi Association), they met the demands of a vast price-sensitive Indian market, and do so even today. Trade in jeans, confectionery, pre-fabricated furniture, paper and textiles are some goods over which this township still has an edge.

In spite of displacement from their homeland in 1947–1948, there were two reasons why the success of this community was almost a certainty.

One, the Sindhi *Bhaiband* (lit. brothers in arms)[17] or Sindh*workis* overseas trading network was well-established *before* India's Partition, which displaced this community from their homeland in Sindh – it became part of Pakistan. The Shikarpuri Sindhis from the land-bound city of Shikarpur, Sindh, in particular, had a pre-colonial global trading and financial network that extended from Astrakhan on the Caspian Sea to the Straits of Malacca. It was this community of merchants and bankers who introduced and popularised the promis-sory note known as the *Hundi* – the main currency used on the Central Asian caravan routes (Agarwal n.d.).

Prior to their travel to British colonies and outposts overseas (that is before Sindh became part of British India in 1843), the Shikarpuris were active on the Eurasian caravan trade routes. This network was dealt a blow by the Great Game (late 19th century) in Central Asia by the competing powers of Imperial Russia and Great Britain, jostling for influence in Central and South Asia. And ultimately by the Russian Revolution when many Shikarpuris were ruined, as they had large holdings of Russian Roubles (Bhavnani 2014).

With the decline of Shikarpur, this network of trade, credit and a rich portfolio of local products shifted to Hyderabad, the capital city of the Baluchi Talpur Amirs (rulers of Sindh). This gave rise to new overseas networks, connecting colonial port cities. French Historian Claude Markovits describes it as the most extensive of all Indian merchant networks abroad, which around 1947, stretched from Kobe in Japan to Panama, with several firms having branches in all the major ports along the two main sea-routes, Bombay-Kobe (via Colombo, Singapore, Surabaya, Saigon, Canton, Shanghai, Manila) and Bombay-Panama (via Port-Sudan, Port Said, Alexandria, Valletta, Gibraltar, Tenerife, or alternatively via Lourenco-Marques, Cape Town, Freetown). By 1937, it was estimated that there were 5000 of these Sindhworkis, who specialised in the sale of silk and curios, scattered across the world (Markovits 2009).

Initially, with the Central Asian markets disrupted by political instability in the late 19th century, and native kingdoms impoverished by British rule, they began selling 'Sindh work' (ivory, wood and enamel carving, lacquer work, textiles and embroidery made by Sindhi Muslim artisans) to British soldiers, who turned out to be a ready market: they called them the Sindhworkis.

Before Partition, the men travelled for two or three years, leaving their families home. Often, there was a *Sethia* (boss), who set out with a group of young men from his family and an extended friends' circle. They traded across the seas, meeting not just the demand for Sindh work, but selling Malta lace in Japan, and vice versa: Japanese curios in Malta.

Second, it was on this bedrock of relatives abroad, along with home-grown success stories from the camps themselves (like the owners of the Colaba-headquartered Kailash Parbat restaurants, who once lived in the Kalyan Camp), who donated towards educational, social, business and community infrastructure within the camps, which helped the community to succeed under challenging conditions.

Many of the young men left the camps to seek their fortunes abroad, only returning to collect their families, where once the norm pre-Partition was to leave families behind in Sindh. Of those who stayed behind, many have flourished in the numerous home and cottage, small- and medium-scale manufacturing units and trading businesses in Ulhasnagar that now service the Indian market.

The Sindhi contribution to Bombay city itself is enormous. Much after the imprint left by 19th- and early 20th-century merchant philanthropists, such as Jamsetjee Jeejeebhoy, and prior to the corporate social responsibility (CSR) practised today, was the establishment from the 1950s to 1980s of Sindhi hospitals, like Jaslok and Hinduja, and educational institutions, such as Jaihind, Kishinchand Chellaram and National College.

The Sindhis are also attributed with popularising the concept of the co-operative housing society in Bombay. In 1914, Bombay got its first residential co-operative society at Gamdevi pioneered by Rao Bahadur S. S. Talmaki, a Maharashtrian, but Sindhi housing societies, like Navjivan Society, and Nanik Niwas and Shyam Niwas at Warden Road, which were all built during the 1950s, set up a new paradigm for community housing. Bombay had been dominated until then by the tenancy model (Bhavnani 2014).

Ulhasnagar, and its parent city of Mumbai, is rightfully called 'mini Sindh' because this city is today the headquarters of a community with a worldwide presence.

Just like the Bhatia, Khoja, Bohra and Sindhi communities, Mumbai is home to numerous trading communities like the Lohana and the Memon, all of who were attracted to the city for its opportunities, commercial services, security and religious tolerance. They all adopted Bombay as their home by building a religious, social, educational and business ecosystem so that they could pursue their livelihoods and their faith here in the safety of British Bombay, and after Partition, in India's financial capital, biggest port and most cosmopolitan city. For the most part, Bombay never failed them – however humble their beginnings in that city.

Moreover, there was always the opportunity to travel overseas using the goodwill of their community or town/village networks. Most Indian overseas communities established themselves in British colonies abroad, with the exception of the early wave of immigrants in the 17th century, who settled in Omani territories in the Middle East and East Africa, often travelling there through the Kutch port of Mandvi. It is easy to forget in the overwhelmingly colonial narrative of history that the Omanis were once a power in the Indian Ocean and strong enough to reassert former Arab hegemony vis-à-vis the Portuguese control of the Indian Ocean shipping routes.

Notes

1 The Mrima coast lies roughly on the coastal mainland opposite Zanzibar Island and the Pemba archipelago (north of Zanzibar).

2 Geo-strategically, the Portuguese controlled this coast for 100 years, but their power over this vast region declined over time. It was the Omani Arabs who first seriously challenged Portuguese dominion in the Indian Ocean arena, much before other Europeans did. Among Asiatic naval powers, they were not the first to do, but had a far more lasting success in ousting the Portuguese than the Ottoman navy and the Safavids of Persia.

3 Before the rise of Surat from late 16th century, Jain merchants were concentrated in Porbandar, Jamnagar, Diu and Cambay, from where they exported cotton piece goods, indigo, wheat and rice to Hormuz, Mocha, Jiddah (Jeddah), Muscat, Aden, Zanzibar and Kilwa. In fact, the *Kiswahili* terms *Bafta* and *Kaniki*, which are still in use today, have their origins in local Gujarati names for particular types of cloth.

4 As Karimjee Jivanjee & Co. was based in German Tanganyika, it forced the closure of their operations in Bombay during the Second World War. They never re-opened their office after the War.

5 The Mariwala family of Bombay is famous for their Parachute coconut oil brand.

6 Some prominent Bhatia textile mill-owners are the Khatau (Khatau mills), Morarji Gokuldas (Morarji Gokuldas Mills and also owners of the Scindia Steamship Co.) and Dharamsey Thackersey (Thackersey Mills) families.

7 The Aga Khan does not consider his work as philanthropy but as his spiritual mandate. In the understanding of Imamate (office of Imam), the Imam (in this context the Aga Khan) is responsible for the improvement in the quality of life of his followers and also those among who they live and are in need.

8 Prior to 1935, Iran was known as Persia. At the time Aga Khan I immigrated to Bombay, it was Persia.

9 The first case of 1847 concerned female rights of inheritance to property, and whether in the case of Ismailis, it was governed by customary law or Sharia (Islamic Law). The second case, the Great Khoja Case (1851), a reform group (Barbhais or 12 Brethrens) challenged the authority of the Aga Khan.

10 Today, the Ismailis worldwide have national councils for each country, and depending on the size of the community, the number of administrative layers is determined.

11 German Tanganyika is today's Tanzania, except that Zanzibar is part of Tanzania today while this wasn't the case during the colonial period.

12 By 1873, British India Steam Navigation Company was running a regular steamer service between Bombay and East Africa.

13 It was the 45th Dai, Syedna Tayyeb Zainuddin, who was appointed to Bombay's Legislative council in 1824–1825.

14 The Omani Sultan's dominions of Zanzibar, Pemba and the mainland Mrima coast became part of the British colony in East Africa.

15 Belgian Congo became Rwanda.

16 The GIPR has been renamed the Central Railway and is headquartered at Chhatrapati Shivaji Terminus (formerly Victoria Terminus or VT). The BB&CI is today Western Railway and has its headquarters at the former BB&CI building opposite Churchgate Station.

17 The Sindhis are classified not by caste but by profession. The Amils, or Sindhi Hindus who belong to the educated segment of the pervasive Lohana caste (although there are tribals and other groupings too), are largely from Hyderabad, Sindh. Hyderabad, Sindh, was the former capital of Sindh and the educational and cultural hub of the Sindh Province. It was the British who shifted the provincial capital from Hyderabad to Karachi. The Amils were treasurers and book-keepers to the Balochi Talpur rulers of Sindh. When Sindh came under the EEIC in 1843, they took up key posts as administrators in the colonial government.

Bibliography

Agarwal, Saaz. n.d. *The Sindhworkis Unique Global Diaspora*. Accessed August, 2016. https://www.sahapedia.org/the-sindhworkis-unique-global-diaspora.

Aim25. n.d. *Mackinnon, Sir William, 1st Baronet*. Accessed May 26, 2016. http://www.aim25.ac.uk/cgi-bin/search2?coll_id=149&inst_id=19.

Asians, Ugandan. 2011. *Allidina Visram (1851–1916)*. June. Accessed May 26, 2016. https://ismailimail.files. wordpress.com/2011/06/allidina-visram-pgs.pdf.

Bhanuben, Kotecha, Leynore Reynell. n.d. *On The Threshold Of East Africa*. The Jyotiben Madhvani Foundation.

Bhavnani, Nandita. 2014. *The Making of Exile: Sindhi Hindus and the Partition of India*. New Delhi: Tranquebar Press.

Daftary, Farhad. 2011. *A Modern History of the Ismailis: Continuity and Change in a Muslim Community*, by Farhad Daftary Ed. London: I.B. Taurus Publishers in association with The Institute of Ismaili Studies.

Edwardes, S.M., 1909. *The Gazetteer of Bombay City And Island. 1977*. Vol. 2. Bombay: Gazetteer Department Government of Maharashtra.

Feeroz, Mustafa, interview by Lentin Sifra. 2020. *History of the Bombay Bohra Community* (October 23).

Group, The Mehta. n.d. *History of the Mehta Group*. Accessed May, 2016. http://www.mehtagroup.com/history.html#.

Hardas, Makhijaa, interview by Lentin Sifra. 2017. *Sindhi Refugees in Kalyan Camp* (August 19).

Hatim, Amiji. 1975. "The Bohras of East Africa." *Journal of Religion in East Africa*, Vol. VII, 27–61.

Herdeck, Margaret, Piramal Gita. 1985. *India's Industrialists: Volume 1*. London: Boulder & London.

n.d. "Iftitah Bina al Masjid al Badri al Hani." pg. 9.

IIS. 2015. *About Us: His Highness Aga Khan*. July 6. Accessed July 13, 2017. https://www.iis.ac.uk/about-us/his-highness-aga-khan/ismaili-imamat-history.

Kaplan, Robert D. 2011. *Monsoon: The Indian Ocean And The Future Of American Power*. New York: Random House Trade Paperbacks.

Khimji, Devyani Gulabsi, interview by Lentin Sifra. 2015. *Omani Bhatia community* (June 27).

Lentin, Sifra. 2020. *Afghan Hindus & Sikhs under attack*. April 2. https://www.gatewayhouse.in/afghan-hindus-sikhs.

Madhvani, Manubhai, Giles Foden. 2009. *Tide of Fortune: A Family Tale*. New Delhi: Random House India.

Markovits, Claude. 2009. *The Global World of Indian Merchants, 1750-1947: Traders of Sind from Bukhara to Panama*. Cambridge: Cambridge University Press.

Mehta, Makarand. 2001 (Updated 2018). "Gujarati Business Communities In East African Diaspora." *Economic and Political Weekly* (Economic & Political) 36 (20). Accessed January 2020.

Mehta, Nanji Kalidas. 1987. *Dream Half Expressed: An Autobiography*. Raj Ratna Nanjibhai Kalidas Mehta Centenary Celebration Committee.

Metcalf, Thomas R. 2008. *Imperial Connections: India In The Indian Ocean Arena, 1860–1920*. Berkeley and Los Angeles: University of California Press.

Oonk, Gijsbert. 2009. *The Karimjee Jivanjee Family: Merchant Princes of East Africa 1800–2000*. Amsterdam: Amsterdam University Press.

Roland, Oliver, Gervase Mathew. 1963. *History Of East Africa Volume One*. London: The Colonial Office.

S.M., Edwardes. 1909. *The Gazetteer of Bombay City And Island. Vol. 2.* 3 vols. Bombay: Reprint Edition The Executive Editor and Secretary Gazetteer Department, Government of Maharashtra.

Sheriff, Abdul. 2002. *Slaves, Spices & Ivory in Zanzibar: Integration of an East African Commercial Empire into the World Economy, 1770–1873.* U.K.: James Currey.

4 Émigrés of the Bombay Presidency

In Chapter 3, we explored how Bombay attracted a host of internal migrant trading communities from its hinterland. The later migrants – Hindu Sindhi refugees – arrived in the aftermath of India's Partition in 1947, choosing to settle as close as they possibly could to the island city because it afforded the opportunities to rebuild their lives. Most succeeded, a few didn't, and many used it as a transit point to seek their fortunes overseas or for families to join their menfolk, who were already a part of the overseas *Sindhworkies* network. These internal migrants, whilst creating overseas networks, are still a sizeable presence in the city and its extended Mumbai Metropolitan Region (MMR).

In stark contrast is the residual presence of once flourishing foreign trading communities – the Baghdadi Jews, Armenians, Turks, Iranians, Pathans, Chinese and Japanese communities – whose religious markers (places of worship, cemeteries) and institutions are the only reminders of their once vibrant presence. The arrival of these communities (with the exception of the Japanese) coincided with that of the internal trading communities, in the 18th and 19th centuries. Japanese expatriates began arriving in large numbers only in the early 20th century, as did the Europeans, most notably the Germans, the French and the Italians, all of who had a sizeable stake in the trade between Bombay and their countries. This was also evident by the presence of their diplomatic missions (see chapter 6), banks and shipping companies in Bombay.

It was colonial Bombay and its Presidency's expanding trade and political influence over vast swathes of Asia – at first its traditional export markets in the Persian Gulf (Muscat, Basra-Baghdad, Gombroon and Bushire)[1] and the littoral regions of the Red Sea (Aden and the Haj market at Jiddah) – and then the Far East (Imperial China and Imperial Japan), and in the late 19th century into Continental Europe and the United States, that attracted foreign trading communities to the city. Bombay's growing preeminence as a

DOI: 10.4324/9781003182894-4

major shipping and transshipment node, and international financial centre, albeit a colonial one, was the result of a coalescing global economy brought about by European colonialism.

This global economy began sometime in 1870 with the opening of the Suez Canal, which shortened the direct shipping route from Bombay to Europe to about 30 days from three to four months (depending on the number of en route victualling stops). Better and faster travel and connectivity – like the telegraph service between London and Calcutta of 1870 – integrated global markets further, thereby enabling more and faster transactions.

In detailing the history of foreign traders in Bombay, this chapter highlights the human and community experiences in this city of trade. Every community has its own unique story. It is through their places of worship, their cemeteries, community halls, schools, charities, printing presses and businesses that we draw out the merchant-community leaders, and who in turn attracted more of their kinsmen to the city with promises of work or by the example of their success.

It is the foreign traders who traversed the ancient *dhow* trade routes of Bombay-Basra/Baghdad and Bushire (Bandar Bushehr), who were the earliest settlers in EEIC Bombay.

The Baghdad–Basra and Bombay connections

The Baghdadi Jewish merchant community from Surat were part of the two millennia old Indian Ocean *dhow* coastal trading networks, which stretched all the way to the Mediterranean ports[2] (Rachel 2013). These merchants traded in just about everything from textiles, brassware, metals, indigo, candy, spices, bullion, pearls and gems, not just with the Middle East and the Mediterranean but also with the East – the port cities of the Bay of Bengal, the Straits of Malacca, Indonesia, Siam (Thailand), Tonkin (Vietnam), China and Japan.

They were known to trade at the port city of Surat almost since it was conquered in 1572 by Emperor Akbar and brought under Mughal rule. What is notable about the Surat traders was that they are amongst the earliest known (so far) Jewish merchant[3] settlement on the Subcontinent, as their kinsmen before them were sojourners. They brought their families with them, and established a synagogue and a cemetery (still existing) in Surat.

Like the Baghdadi Jewish traders, there were other West Asian émigré merchants in Surat, like the Armenians (from New Julfa in Persia), the Arabs, Persian Shia merchants and the Turks, all communities, who like the Baghdadi Jews, migrated to and had a presence in Bombay. These foreign traders settled in EEIC Bombay because of the deteriorating security, economic and political decline of Surat after the death of Emperor Aurangzeb in 1707.

Another aspect of their migration to Bombay were the interactions of these foreign community networks with the commercial residents of the EEIC, at first in Gombroon (Bandar Abbas), where the Company had a factory,[4] then later at Basra, where the Company's Gombroon factory was shifted in 1763 due to political difficulties, and even later to Baghdad which had an English political resident from 1798 (Yapp 1967). The establishment of an EEIC diplomatic mission at Baghdad (then part of the Ottoman Empire), according to one study, marked a shift in policy to the political sphere from the commercial, and a marked divergence from England's foreign policy then. Be that as it may, these points of contacts between West Asian overseas traders and Company residents at these ports seem to point to active encouragement of these communities to settle in colonial Bombay. The Basra–Bombay trade, well-known for its pearls and horses, was not only one of the busiest routes but well-established because Basra was also a nodal point for the mail service to and from Bombay to England.[5]

Trade and community: patterns of settlement in Bombay

The first settler in Bombay from the Baghdadi Jewish community is believed to be the Surat merchant Joseph Semah in about 1730 (Roland 1998; Edwardes 1909). The 18th century was also a time when the Armenian, Persian, Arab and Turkish traders were also a thin presence in the city, much like the Jewish traders, as Surat remained an important port despite the challenges it faced. In the case of the Baghdadi community, what triggered direct immigration from West Asia into Bombay was the persecution of the Jews in Baghdad by the cruel Turkish *Wali* (governor) Daud Pasha [6] from 1817 to 1831. The forceable conversion of the Meshed Jews of Persia in 1839 made this community too seek refuge in Bombay.

The immigration of David Sassoon, who was the traditional *Nasi* (spiritual) and temporal head of the Baghdadi Jews, to Bombay in 1832, resulted in an increasing number from this community coming to the city. Sassoon had a growing need for employees as his business – he was a banker and trader – began flourishing as soon as he settled in the city. His building of community institutions ensured a religious-cultural framework for community life.

On his arrival in the city, David Sassoon nailed a *Mezuzah* (a sign of a Jewish home) on the doorpost of his first home at 9 Tamarind Lane within the Fort. It is unclear, where the early Baghdadi merchants were settled within the city but before the arrival of Sassoon, they worshipped at the *Shaar Harahamim* (Gate of Mercy) synagogue (est. 1796) – a Bene Israel synagogue – on Samuel Street.

David Sassoon continued to trade in the region he knew best – West Asia. His oldest son Abdullah (better known as Sir Albert Sassoon) earned his spurs in this region, when he was sent there to meet the family's business contacts. West Asia continued to remain Sir Albert's area of expertise even after the Sassoons expanded their businesses to the Far East and ventured into manufacturing – they owned the largest number of textile mills in Bombay and employed about 15,000 workers. It was the manpower that Sassoon sourced to work in Sassoon businesses in the early years, whether at 9 Tamarind Lane, David Sassoon & Sons, his warehouses, and as travelling overseas agents, many were largely his kinsmen. Some renowned Jewish families in the Far East, like the Hong Kong based Sir Elly Kadoorie family, and the Shanghai real estate giant of the 1920s–1930s – Silas Hardoon – were Baghdadi Jews who first trained at Sassoon headquarters in Bombay before being posted overseas.

Sassoon began providing for the accommodation, religious needs, schooling of his kinsmen, and this formed the core of a geospatial settlement pattern for this Middle-Eastern Jewish community in the city. Like the Marathi-speaking Bene-Israel, then concentrated in the vicinity of their synagogue on Samuel Street (Mandvi), the Baghdadis too lived close to their synagogue[7] – the *Magen David* (lit. Star of David) synagogue built by Sassoon in 1861 – in Byculla, and in adjoining Nagpada. David Sassoon's own palatial home *Sans Souci* (today's Masina Hospital) was also in Byculla, and is located close to this synagogue.

Whilst the prosperity and growth of this Jewish community in Bombay, during the second half of the 19th century, is closely aligned to its foremost merchant and his two oldest sons – Abdullah (Albert) and Elias – who parted ways after their father's death in 1864, with Elias establishing his own businesses under the banner of E.D. Sassoon & Co. It is from Bombay, where both Sassoon firms – old and new – were initially headquartered,[8] that they expanded their businesses to England, China, British Hong Kong and Japan. Both also carried forward their father's philanthropic work as is evident in the numerous Sassoon endowments – charitable, institutional (schools, hospitals) and ceremonial,[9] all of which are still functional and visible even today.

By the late 19th century, the more well-off among the Baghdadi community (many businessmen) shifted to a new precinct of the city – Colaba – which was in close proximity to the Sir Jacob Sassoon endowed Keneseth Eliyahoo Synagogue (est. 1884).

Compared to the well-known presence of the Sassoons' and their kinsmen is the little-known small Iranian Shia merchant community, whose roots in the city go back almost 200 years. These businessmen, who form a part of the 2,500 Iranian Shias in Mumbai today, have been less visible than their fellowmen from Yazd – as also the Irani Zoroastrians also from Yazd – who came much after them but enjoy instant recognition as owners of Bombay's popular Irani cafés.

While the café owners were originally from the smaller towns of south-central Iran (Yazd and Kerman), the merchant community hail mainly from port cities like Bushire (Bandar Bushehr), and urban cultural hubs like Shiraz, Isfahan and Kashan that were connected to it. The earliest among the Iranian Shias to settle in colonial Bombay chose Dongri in central Bombay as their base because it was close to the city's dockyards.

Many of the Bombay families are from Shiraz (Jalali Sayed 2019), a city whose merchants supplied goods such as carpets woven especially for the export markets, and offered finance and commercial know-how to the nearest port of Bushire. Bushire had a British resident since 1763, who reported directly to the governor in Bombay. The British Residency here, which had a factory, facilitated trade mainly between the Presidency of Bombay and Persia[10] (political residency bushire n.d.).

There are also a few families in Mumbai, whose roots are in Persian merchant settlements in non-Iranian regions of the Gulf, like Basra and Bahrain, whose forefathers too came to Bombay to participate in the Persian Gulf trade with Bombay during the 19th and early 20th centuries, just like the Arabs from this region, and the Afghan traders from Kandahar. Nineteenth-century Bombay was the epoch of the trade in horses, and Arab, Persian and Kandahar merchants were all involved in their large-scale supply to the British Indian Army and Bombay's horse-drawn tramway services, which commenced in 1874.[11]

Horses apart, the Persian merchants' import manifests included dried fruits, *attar* (floral oils), Shiraz wine, curios and some articles of luxury, such as books, embroidered slippers and silk shawls (Edwardes 1909). From Bombay to Persia went rice, ghee, teakwood, spices, sugar, indigo and textiles, both British and Indian mill-made.

The eponymous Haji Ebrahim Busheri's rise to prosperity mirrors this narrative. Originally from the port of Bushire, he arrived in the city in the early 1850s as an 18-year-old (Durazi and Daruwala 2019). He began by trading in dried fruits, then expanded into real estate, owning many buildings in Dongri, where he lived. By 1910, he was wealthy enough to build a palatial family bungalow in Bandra. Busheri's great-grandchildren from their paternal side are Durazi's, a well-known Bombay family. Their surname indicates that they are half Iranian and half Bahrainian, as Duraz derives from a town in Bahrain: their paternal grandfather was a pearl diver and trader, and Bombay was the largest pearl market east of the Suez: he too eventually settled in the city.

Some figures point to the feverishness with which trade between Bombay and Persia grew. In 1830, the total trade between the two countries was Rs. 350,000, and by 1859, the annual trade in horses alone had risen to Rs. 2,625,000 (Mohiuddin and Poonawala 2009). Consequently, by 1865, the number of Iranians officially registered as residing in Bombay was 1,639 (Bombay Almanac and Directory 1865).

The city's commercial prominence led to the establishment of a permanent Persian consulate in Bombay in the early half of the 19th century (Nile 2011). And by 1919, the Imperial Bank of Persia had opened one of its few overseas branches in the city.[12]

A major responsibility for the Persian consul then was overseeing Haj pilgrims from Persia, who disembarked first in Bombay before taking a ship to Jiddah. The ships from Bushire and Bandar Abbas (Gombroon) carried goods, merchants and Haj pilgrims, but also, unexpectedly enough, mendicants and Iranian Sufi preachers, many of whom were merchants. The latter two groups were drawn to Bombay by the famed generosity of its wealthy Iranian merchants, and the more recent arrival of their countryman and political refugee, the Ismaili Khoja spiritual head, Aga Khan I and his family in 1848.

This mix of Iranian settlers and visitors invariably converged on Imambada Road's turquoise blue Irani Masjid, which was established in 1860. Known locally as 'Mughal Masjid', community members clarify that the term 'Mughal' actually refers to the fact of Persian being adopted as the official language of the Mughal court, where many Persian poets, intellectuals and artists took up residence from the time of Emperor Akbar's reign through that of Jahangir and Shah Jahan.

The donor of this magnificent mosque was *Malik al-tujjar* Haj Muhammed Husayn Shirazi, whose title indicates that he held the semi-formal office of leader of the Iranian merchants in the city. It was here, in the vicinity of this mosque, that the Persian merchants of the 19th and early 20th centuries set up a religious, social and educational institutional ecosystem that sustained Shia migrants and visitors. Celebrated Sufi preacher from Isfahan, Safi `Ali Shah, who arrived in Bombay in 1864, recalled that on arrival, he was out on his luck, with no money or contacts in the city, and had to seek accommodation in a small house on the Irani Masjid's *waqf* property, one of several rooms either inside or adjoining the Masjid, built specifically for poor itinerant visitors (Nile 2011). All such donors were merchants, who established one mosque, a school – the Amin School, which doubles as an *imambara* (hall) during Moharram – and an *anjuman* (community hall), all in close proximity to the Irani Masjid.[13] This is the heart of Shia Mumbai even today, as the name of the road itself is a reference to the four *imambaras*, located just off it, namely Amin, Sostori, Nemāzī and Darbār-e-Ḥosaynī.

The Iranian community congregates at the Amin Imambara during Moharram when special preachers and *mullahs* are brought down from Qom to conduct the *Majlis* (Moharram) sermons in Farsi (Persian). Another Iranian tradition that the early merchants brought to Bombay is the dramatic enactment of the Battle of Karbala and the martyrdom of Imam Husain in 680 AD, complete with ritual self-flagellation, on the final day of Moharram.

The Iranian Shias and Zoroastrians may have different religions, but they share a language and culture that goes back two millennia and much before the Arab conquest of the pre-Islamic Sassanid Empire in the 7th century AD. For example, the Iranian New Year – *Nauruz* – on March 21 (the Spring Equinox) is celebrated by both communities, including the Parsis, their predecessors in the Indian subcontinent, for whom it is the spring festival.

Afghan traders in Bombay

Another transnational émigré network in the city is the tribal Afghan or **Pathan** trading community. This community is considered by many as indigenous to the Indian subcontinent, as most hail from the former British Indian North West Frontier Province (which included the princely kingdom of Swat) and Federally Administered Tribal Areas (FATA), or today's Khyber Pakhtunkhwa Province (KPP) in neighbouring Pakistan. The tribes[14] that came under the influence of the Indian subcontinent lay east of the Durand Line and west of the Indus River, a natural marker for the beginning of Pathan terrain: they were the Eastern Pathans who came from the Peshawar Plain and valleys to its north, as well as highlanders from the mountainous regions of the Pamir, Hindukush and the Sulaiman (north Baluchistan), who speak Pushto or its northern, gruffer variant, written in the Dari script. Those to the west came under the Persian influence and speak Dari, a variant of Farsi.

With their ancestral lands lying in Pakistan, this has created problems for Mumbai's Pathans, as those who opted for Indian citizenship, being multi-generational residents in the city, are finding it increasingly difficult to travel freely across borders that were once delineated either as a strategic buffer in the Great Game between Imperial Russia and Great Britain, or outlined for administrative purposes. About 400 still retain their Residential Permits (RPs) even today (Rao 2019).[15]

Earlier Pathan tribes on either side of the Durand Line border between Afghanistan and British India could travel freely. Traders, labourers, visiting relatives and brides would cross and re-cross this border. Even after India's Partition, it was relatively easy to enter India from Pakistan and vice versa, till recently. In spite of these impediments, Pathans born in India and holding an Indian passport, often travel from the city to their home villages in the Afghan belt of Pakistan to get married and bring their bride back to India. A tradition that continues to date.

Reverse migrations occur too. A Bombay-born and raised Pathan recently married two of his daughters into families settled in Karachi and Kabul. This has kept the community's centuries-old transnational network as active as it ever was, facilitating a way of life, especially the preference to marry within the tribe (Caroe 1958).

The Afghan or Pathan merchants' trade with Bombay has historically consisted of the traditional dry fruits and saffron – import, wholesale and retail – and is something that they are still engaged in, as it constitutes 62% of the total trade between Afghanistan and India, as per the 2018–2019 trade data (Sarwari 2019). In recent years though, Pathan businessmen have found the import–export business in gemstones – lapis lazuli, rubies and emeralds – also proving lucrative, as these gemstones are imported into India (mostly Rajasthan) for value addition like cutting, polishing and setting, and then re-exported.

The Afghan merchant's trade with the Indian subcontinent, and even Bombay in the 19th century, has been a predominantly overland trade. Though the route to Calcutta via the Indo-Gangetic plains saw more footprints, as epitomised in Nobel Laureate Rabindranath Tagore's iconic story *Kabuliwallah,* which showcases how commonplace it was then in Calcutta for Afghan dry fruit peddlers to sell their wares from home to home. In Bombay too, there are references to the Afghan–Bombay trade, with the well-known merchant David Sassoon acting as banker, money-lender to, and purchaser of goods brought to the city by Afghan caravan traders. Another iconic Bombay *Sethia* of the 19th century, who acted as banker to these merchants, was Jaganath Shankarsett.

It is because of the imperatives of oral history regarding their origins, a maze of tribal genealogies and feuds, and the realities of geopolitics – since their homeland has historically been a zone of conflict and situated at the crossroads of trade, the China-Pakistan Economic Corridor running through Pathan villages – makes them hardy as a people and the need to maintain their cultural identity urgent.

One Mumbai Afghan shopowner's take on why the Afghans are particular about protecting their cultural identity wherever they are; today many work in blue-collar jobs in the Gulf countries, like they once used to in the dockyards, petroleum refineries in Trombay, or as security guards in Bombay's textile mills and at the mill-owners' bungalows on Malabar Hill. He reasons that his community prefers to be low-key, and just want to maintain their culture, religion and way of life wherever they happen to be located. They do not like to involve themselves in politics as almost everyone in Mumbai have family in KPP in Pakistan and on the other side of the border in Afghanistan. Besides, because of a highly strung and almost tactile transnational feudal network, information too tends to get distorted. Misunderstandings can occur when this happens. Hence, most Pathans tend to be secretive even within their immediate families about business, in particular, in order to guard against jealousy, extortion and tribal feuds back home in their ancestral villages.

With Bombay's mills having given way to plush commercial spaces – the community is no longer as visible as before. They still inhabit the *Saat Rasta* (Jacob Circle) precinct in Central Mumbai and Fort, such as the areas adjacent to Ballard Pier, with its parallel streets full of warehouses close to the docks.

What really places Mumbai's Pathan in the spotlight today are the Pathan film stars – past and present – like Dilip Kumar (Yousuf Khan), Jayant (Zakariya Khan) and his sons Amjad and Imtiaz Khan, the brothers Feroz (Zulfikar Ali) – Sanjay (Shah Abbas)-Akbar Khan, and today's superstars Shah Rukh Khan, Salman Khan and Aamir Khan. Famous scriptwriter Salim Khan, who hails from Indore, where his great-great grandfather settled after immigrating from the Swat region, began his career as an actor but shone in his award-winning partnership of 16 years with Javed Akhtar. This larger-than-life imprint of the Pathan on Bombay's Hindi film industry, whose films have a global reach and whose stars are household names across South, Central Asia and large parts of West Asia, can in some way be traced back to their roots: most are multilingual, coming from regions which were at the crossroads of civilisation and trade. Therefore, their entry into the Bombay film industry at a time when it was making its transition into the talkies era was fortuitous. The opportunities to leverage this Hindi film connect between Bombay and Afghanistan, where three major films – *Dharmatma* (1975), *Khuda Gawah* (1992) and *Kabul Express* (2006) – have already been shot, are vast. This is even more so given the positive soft diplomacy and trade bilateral relationship between the two countries.

Looking East: China and Japan

Bombay's trade with the Arabian Sea littoral was older not only because of its proximity to the Gulf region and the Arabian Peninsula but also because the late medieval trading networks and communities from these regions extended their businesses to Bombay from Surat, with many relocating to the city by the 19th century.

In comparison to this, the trade between Bombay and Imperial China was relatively new, beginning sometime in 1730s (Edwardes 1909) with that great white staple – cotton – from the Deccan, when southern China experienced a severe drought and an Imperial edict soon mandated that only food crops could be sown in the next season. Whilst the foundations of the Bombay–Canton trade were being established by the Agency Houses and Bombay's merchants (see Chapter 3), there was no reciprocal presence of Chinese traders (Imperial China permitted only limited access to foreign trading companies at its port of Canton, today's Guangzhou) or workers, in colonial Bombay.[16]

Though there is no confirmed date when the Chinese community first settled in Bombay, there are two milestones that point to the second half of the 19th century. There is a Chinese cemetery atop Antop Hill (Sewri); five Chinese merchants bought the land for it on 10 November 1889 at six annas per yard. It became functional after a boundary wall was erected three months later. The other cemetery, now defunct, is in Kamathipura, central Bombay, a neighbourhood that, at the turn of the 20th century, came to be designated New China Town.

The second milestone is the Chinese Temple on Nawab Tank Road (Mazagaon) dedicated to the legendary Chinese warrior king, Kwan Tai Kung (lit. the Great One), which was consecrated in 1953, but located in a 19th-century building that once housed a Chinese-run marine institute. The connection between these two disparate markers is the immigration of the Tham (Cantonese) clan to Bombay sometime in the second half of the 19th century, *after* Imperial China lost the First Opium War (1839–1842). It was the end of this war that triggered a wave of migration from Canton and adjoining areas to Hong Kong, South East Asia, Calcutta and Bombay. A common surname, like Tham, is indicative of common ancestral roots. Members of a clan not only hail from the same region in China but are also linked together by ethical instructions, passed down through male heirs of successive generations. This meant that the institute was largely for Cantonese Chinese, the dominant group in the early years (Tham 2018).

The caretaker of Bombay's only Chinese temple, Albert Tham, recalls that his grandfather, who spoke very good English and dressed like an Englishman – suit, monocle, walking stick – was a British India Steam Navigation Company (BISN) labour contractor. The present Mazagaon Dockyard Ltd. (MDL) shipyard close to the Temple, so close in fact that one can see its forbidding boundary wall from the Temple, was originally the shipyard for the EEIC, and later for Peninsular & Orient Shipping (P&O) and its BISN Company. To cater to the needs of this shipyard, the Tham clan opened the marine institute on Nawab Tank Road, where migrant Chinese men were trained in ship's carpentry, welding and fitting, so they could work in the dockyards and on ships. Many also learnt cooking and could serve on the BISN passenger ships. In fact, many Chinese were employed even post-Independence in this shipyard that was to becomes MDL, India's premier naval shipyard.

Viewed from a geopolitical lens, the creation of an Indian Chinese diaspora was very much an outcome of colonial circulations of people in the late 18th, 19th and first half of the 20th centuries, which also resulted in the creation of Indian diasporas in the network of colonial ports across the world. But there was one BIG difference between the two diasporas: the Chinese never ventured to Africa or the Gulf region. According to one interviewee (Hsieh 2017), Calcutta was the preferred last port, where you made money and returned. The practicality of this was underscored by a regular steamer service, which made it possible to return home frequently. These early residents were termed 'sojourners' as they often went back home to marry – the steamer service ran between Calcutta and Canton (Guangzhou) and Hong Kong – and also remitted their earnings to their families in China. This practice was common even during the Qing Dynasty and during the Republic of China (1912–1949) (Encyclopaedia Britannica n.d.).

In addition to the Cantonese (who were in large numbers in Bombay's Chinese community), there were also Hakka, Hupei (alternatively Hubei) and Shadong Chinese, whose widely differing dialects indicate the period when these regional clans left China, and the trades they took up during their early years abroad. The latter three groups immigrated in large numbers between 1911 (when the Qing Emperor was deposed) and 1949, when the Chinese Communist Party (CCP) came to power. The Hakka influx was to Calcutta first where they took to shoe-making, leather tanning in Tangra (New China Town), set up bakeries, and their women entered the beauty salon business, a pattern they replicated in Bombay almost completely.

The Hupei, well-known as teeth-setters from central China, came from a region that admitted foreigners only after 1842, settling in Calcutta first. Those from Shadong (a coastal province in East China) were silk peddlers, the region being famous for it.

The reason why these sojourners settled in India is best highlighted by the family history of Baba Ling, Mumbai's well-known Chinese restaurateur and owner of *Ling's Pavilion* (Colaba). Ling remembers his family's migration well: his father, Yick Sen Ling, came to Bombay in 1938 from a village named Santau in the southern province of Canton. Yick Sen with his cousin Chen, and Uncle Ling, opened the first Chinese Museum in the old Cottage Emporium just outside the BEST bus depot on Colaba Causeway (Ling 2017). It was with the establishment of a Communist government in Beijing on 1 October 1949 that the free flow of people, capital and goods into and out of mainland China stopped. This 'marooned' the overseas Chinese, like the Bombay community, who not only lost contact with family and friends in China, but had their landholdings and properties in China confiscated by the Communist government. The Ling family soon closed down the museum as supplies from China became erratic due to the Second World War and civil war in mainland China, and opened Nanking Restaurant in Colaba in 1945, making them today the oldest and third generation Indian Chinese family in the restaurant business in the city.[17]

Unfortunately, this community was dealt a double whammy when war broke out between Communist China and independent India in October 1962. According to the India Census of 1951 and 1961, the population of ethnic Chinese peaked at 9,215 and 14,607, respectively (Ramakrishna 2010), though community members speak of Calcutta alone having a population of about 30,000 Chinese (Tung 2012).[18] The outbreak of war revealed that many multi-generational Indian Chinese were holding resident permits (and not Indian passports), although many were naturalised Indians having been born here. Moreover, those who had taken loans from the erstwhile Bank of China – they were eligible for the loans only if they became Chinese Communist Party card holders – were branded as CCP sympathisers. Most Indian Chinese were interned at Deoli Camp (Rajasthan), with many also imprisoned in local jails on complaints by locals that they were Chinese spies, when in fact it was business rivalry or property grabbing that motivated the complainant. This dreadful experience of entire families in Deoli Camp – the last internees left by 1965–1966 – and in jail, and the fact that most returned to shops and homes that were occupied by trespassers or illegally sold, as was the Chinese school in Star Mansions on Motlibai Street (Agripada, Bombay), impelled this Community to leave India. Half a century later, the Toronto Indian Chinese community, in particular, because of its larger numbers, still retains a cultural affinity with India – be it speaking the language, watching Bollywood movies. The Greater Toronto suburbs of Markham and Scarborough have the largest *Bambaiya* Hindi and Bengali-speaking Indian Chinese community. They have also founded their own clubs and associations. One of these is the Association of Chinese India Deoli Internees, a living reminder of the darkest years in an otherwise unblemished, centuries-old history of the Indian Chinese community.

The Japanese quest for cotton

In contrast, but also in some respects similar to the Chinese immigration, is the once 3,000 strong Japanese expatriate community in Bombay and its Presidency at the turn of the 20th century. This was because of Bombay's buoyant trade with Imperial Japan since 1858, ten years before the Meiji Restoration[19] – until the Second World War brought it all to an end. The city never regained its substantial Japanese resident population, and today it is host to a small community – between 550 and 750 people[20] – when compared to the numbers in Bengaluru, New Delhi, Chennai or India's only Japan Town (Sataku) in Haldia (West Bengal).

In spite of a thin presence, and a lapse of 76 years since the War ended, the history of Bombay's Japanese community is still traceable through some milestones, which have remained hidden from public attention. The history of these markers speaks to us of not just those who arrived to work in the Japanese trading, banking and shipping companies in Bombay but also the *Karayuki San* (lit. Ms Gone Overseas) or young Japanese girls sold into prostitution, first to local procurers by their poor farming or fishing families,[21] and then to overseas brothels. Parallel to this, as in the case of other foreign diasporas, was the circulation of learned men of religion. Numerous Japanese *Bhikshus* (Buddhist monks), many belonging to the Nippozan Myohoji (Japan Buddha Order), travelled to Bombay because of the presence of a community here.

The most enduring vestige of this past is the buff-coloured granite *stambha* (column) in the 111-year-old Japanese cemetery, Nipponjin Boji, on Dr. E. Moses Road (formerly Haines Road),[22] which lists the names of Japanese nationals who came to the city to work in Japanese trading companies, involved in the export of raw cotton and mill-made yarn and import of Japanese cloth. They also worked in banks, in shipping companies, and by the mid-20th century, in manufacturing projects using Japanese technologies. Their ashes are interred at this cemetery, which also has on record those who died while lodged in British Indian prisoner-of-war camps when hostilities broke out between Japan and the Allied Powers in 1941. Some were either locally rounded up or brought from overseas (Yasmin 2015).

The earliest photograph of the Bombay community is of the consecration ceremony of Nipponjin Boji cemetery in 1908 by the Buddhist *Bhikshu* (monk) Gensho Hirota, who wrote of that day, 'I reached Bombay Station and by *ghoda ghari* (horse cart) reached the site [*sic*] where I met Japanese people and, in the evening, I went to the Japanese Gymkhana and did a memorial service'. This photograph also shows several Japanese women, dressed in traditional kimonos, kneeling in prayer. According to Bhikshu Morita San, current caretaker and priest of the Nipponzan Myohoji temple (Worli, Mumbai), who has this photo, a few of them were probably *Karayuki San*. The Karayuki San's migration abroad began a little after Japan opened its ports to foreign trade and the Meiji Restoration of 1868. An interesting aspect of their sojourn in Bombay is that they used it as a nodal hub from which to go west: East Africa, West Africa (Ivory Coast) and California (during the 1910 Gold Rush). From Mumbai, many also migrated into the city's cotton-growing hinterland. In 1908, when the cemetery was opened, there were about 200 Karayuki San and about 600 Japanese in the city (Harald 2003). These numbers were not unusual for Bombay since the global networks of prostitution (including European ones) were centred in colonial port cities and regions such as Shanghai, Hong Kong, Penang, Singapore and Bombay.

A pointed reference to the Japanese community in Bombay is contained in the story of how the idea of setting up a Japan Buddha Order temple in the city came about. The founder of this Order (est. 1917), the Reverend Nichidatsu Fujii – fondly known as Fujii Guruji – arrived in Bombay on 28 November 1931. Following a short spiritual retreat (penance), there is photographic evidence of Fujii Guruji's presence at Ballard Estate pier (Alexandra Docks, today's Indira Docks) on 28 December 1931, amongst the crowds, welcoming Mahatma Gandhi on his return home from the unsuccessful Second Round Table Conference in London.

Two years later on 4 October 1933, Fujii Guruji interacted and stayed with Gandhiji at his Ashram in Wardha (Living with Gandhi:

Rev. Fujii Guruji in India and the Indo-Japanese relations in the 1930s n.d.). It was at this time that his plan to build a Japan Buddha Order temple in India attracted the attention of nationalist businessman and philanthropist J.K. Birla, who eventually endowed the one built in Bombay, though completed belatedly in the 1950s due to the outbreak of the Second World War (San 2019).

The visit of Fujii Guruji coincided with a heightened circulation of people because of trade between the two countries. Japan, especially Yokohama, was the site of the first Indian settlement as early as the 1870s, where the first settlers were a Parsi, named Kumazawa Impuresu (who became a naturalised Japanese), and a Bohra, called Essabhoy (of the firm A.M. Essabhoy). In 1882, the first Sindhi firm – Wassiamull Assomull & Co. – opened an office, also in Yokohama, then a hub for the export of Japanese silk because of its port. They were soon followed by other traders, who unusually, unlike Indian diaspora elsewhere, largely relied on Japanese staff.

Initially, Japan's external trade was dominated by British, European and American trading firms, along with the already established Chinese. Japanese raw silks, teas, handloom textiles, paper, copper, coal and iron were exported, while Chinese, US and Indian cotton yarn, mill-made cloth, woollens and other manufactures were imported. Bombay's big mercantile firms – like Tata and Sassoon firms – and some smaller merchants too, with branches in Chinese port cities, now simply extended their Bombay–China networks into Japan. E.D. Sassoon & Co. was among the first to open a branch in Yokohama soon after the 1858 treaty (Jackson 1968; Overy 2011).

By the 1890s, Japan's external trade saw the entry of the big Japanese firms, like Mitsui Busan (Mitsui Trading Company),[23] which began carrying a greater part of this trade from the period just before the First World War (1914–1918). This began a growing inflow of Japanese staff into Bombay, creating a sizeable community and its sacred, social and cultural spaces, in the early half of the 20th century, something that the Reverend Fujii Guruji witnessed.

The entry of Mitsui Busan in 1893 into Bombay was followed the next year by the establishment of Japan's first official mission in India, headed by Consul Dargoro Goh. The Yokohama Specie Bank (YSB) opened its first agency (it became a branch in 1900) (Nishumura 2012) in the city also in 1894.

The 1890s were also a time when increasing amounts of raw (ginned) cotton – as different from just cotton yarn from Bombay's mills – was exported to Japan. This shift was due to the growth in the number of Japanese spinning mills, the first of which was the Osaka Spinning Mill

(1888) which began producing superior yarn – compared to the foreign imports for Japan's textile mills, centred in Kobe-Osaka. This was a turning point, as now, Japan began looking to India and the Asian markets to sell its enormous surplus of finished cloth. It was here that the overseas Indian community, concentrated in Yokohama and Kobe, played a key role, making them valuable not just to these cities' governments but their prefectures of Kanagawa and Hyogo.

While the British and European companies and big multinational firms traded in large quantities of raw cotton, yarn and indigo with Japan, the Indians settled there leveraged their community networks to market Japanese silks, textiles, pearls, lacquerware, pottery and curios in Shanghai, Hong Kong, Saigon, Manila, Penang, Rangoon, Trincomalee, Calcutta, Bombay and sometimes globally (especially in the case of Sindhi merchants), to the Arabian Peninsula, Africa, Egypt, Gibraltar, Spain and the Americas.

Meanwhile in Bombay, the cotton purchases of Japanese trading firms like Mitsui, Nippon Menkwa Kabushiki Kaisha (Japan Cotton Trading Co. Ltd.),[24] Gosho Kabushiki Kaisha Ltd. and Toyo Menkwa Kaisha Ltd. were financed by a mix of foreign chartered banks (led by the Hong Kong and Shanghai Banking Corporation) and Japanese banks (largely YSB), which worked with the Bank of Bombay's rural branches and even native *shroffs* (bankers) in the cotton hinterland. Japanese buyers in the early years contracted for their cotton consignments through foreign trading houses, but soon ventured into the cotton-growing areas themselves to contract for the crop directly with farmers (Aroon 1994) in the states of the Deccan Plateau, namely, today's southern Gujarat, central Maharashtra, Karnataka and Tamil Nadu.[25] By 1922–1923, they dealt with 30% of India's cotton exports, even selling it in Europe and China.

This led to collaborations – Tata Shipping Lines and Nippon Yusen Kaisha (NYK) in 1893, which lasted a year – and, probably, the first Japanese investment in the Bombay's textile industry: the Toyo Poddar Cotton Mills Ltd. This first Japanese manufacturing facility in the city leveraged Japanese textile technology and management ethics as against an all pervasive British one. There probably would have been more Indo-Japanese joint ventures, had it not been for the outbreak of the Second World War, which began in the Pacific theatre with Japan's invasion of China in 1937.

The war disrupted the Bombay–Japan ties completely, with Japanese manpower (and their families) being either shipped home (if they were lucky to escape in time) or confined in POW camps. It led to

Japanese properties in the city also being confiscated as enemy property, like the Japanese Temple at Worli was.

After the war, business between the two countries resumed with the visit of a Japanese trade mission to Bombay in 1948, to purchase cotton. This was followed by significant Indo-Japanese joint ventures with private partners like Pilot Fountain Pens (1954), Taiyo Fisheries (1954), Eagle Flasks (1955) and Asahi Glass (1956). When Japan changed its development model in 1955, prioritising heavy industries (like iron and steel) and chemicals, its business activities moved from Bombay to Goa – iron ore exports to Japan peaked in the 1960s – and later Delhi, with the 1980s joint venture between Suzuki Motor Corporation and the Indian government assuming prominence. More recently, Bengaluru has been attracting Japanese hi-tech companies to its own businesses and start-ups, as is Chennai, with about 500 Japanese manufacturing companies established in its vicinity.

The immigration of Japanese personnel as history shows, is dictated by where large Japanese trading, manufacturing and start-ups are located, Mumbai and its State of Maharashtra appear to be left behind as indicated by the small numbers from this community resident in the city.

In fact, the presence of all the foreign immigrant communities described in this chapter – Baghdadi Jews, Iranian Shias, Pathans, the Chinese and Japanese – is small. Each community has left its own legacy in Mumbai through its own unique economic, social, religious and cultural contribution to this city. This – as described – is most visible and palpable in the sacred, social and cultural spaces of these communities. The older trading communities – Baghdadis, Persians and Pathans – made their way to the city by extending their age-old trading networks into colonial Bombay. Newer immigrants, Chinese and Japanese, were motivated by the opportunities and the security that Bombay the colonial port city had to offer.

Notes

1 The modern names of Gombroon and Bushire are Bandar Abbas and Bandar Bushehr, respectively.
2 The term 'Baghdadi Jews' has been used by scholars in a generic way. It includes Sephardic Jewish communities across West Asia and North Africa, like those from Egypt, Tunisia and Morocco.
3 Two oldest Jewish communities on the Subcontinent are the Bene Israel (lit. Children of Israel) from the Konkan Coast and the Malabar Jews.
4 A trading establishment at a foreign port was known as a factory. It doubled up as an office, warehouse and sometimes place of residence for foreign merchants.

5 The resident at Basra had to organise a section of the part overland-and-sea mail service between England and Bombay. When the Egyptian route became insecure, it was replaced by a route from Istanbul to Aleppo, then across the desert to Basra, and by sea from Basra to Bombay.

6 Baghdad was then part of the Ottoman Empire. The Ottoman Empire was at its height during the 16th–17th century, and was finally dissolved after the First World War. This dissolution resulted in the creation of new nation states like Egypt, Iraq and Saudi Arabia.

7 Orthodox and conservative Jews prefer to live within walking distance of a synagogue.

8 David Sassoon & Sons, later David Sassoon & Co., shifted their headquarters to London in the late 19th century, while E.D. Sassoon & Co. first transferred their headquarters to Shanghai just before India's independence and then the tax haven of the Bermudas after the Chinese Communist Party's takeover of Shanghai.

9 The most notable are the Gateway of India and the *Kala Ghoda* (a bronze equestrian statue of Prince Edward VII).

10 Initially, the Resident at Bushire reported to the Agent and Council at Basra through whom the whole of his correspondence with the Governor and Council at Bombay was normally channelled. This arrangement lasted until 1778 after which date the status of Basra was reduced from Agency to Residency, and the Resident at Bushire reported directly to Bombay. Bombay continued to be chiefly responsible for the Resident in Bushire till 1873.

11 The electrification of the city's tramways commenced after the incorporation and registration of a new company –Bombay Electric Supply & Tramway (BEST) Company, in London. The first electric tram cars became operational in May 1907.

12 The Imperial Bank of Persia was a British Overseas Bank that between 1889 and 1928 served as a state bank and bank of currency issue for Persia.

13 All these institutions are administered through Trusts run by descendants of these merchant families.

14 The dominant tribes in Bombay – Yusufzai, Hasanzai, Durrani, Shah, Ahmadzai, Kakkad and Afridi (with the exception of the Durrani, also known as Abdali, tribe who hail from the central plains of Afghanistan and to which many Afghan kings belong) all originate from regions that comprise the tribal belts of Pakistan.

15 According to the 1978 Annual Report of the Greater Bombay Police, there were 860 Pathans registered with the Pathan branch of the Special Branch CID Bombay to renew the RPs of the city's Pathan community and mediate in any problems arising with the police. The number of these permits have fallen since to about 400 today, and continue to decline.

16 The first settlement of a Chinese trader and workers is recorded in Calcutta in 1778.

17 The two oldest Chinese restaurants in Bombay, one of them being Lok Jun (1895) on Shuklaji Street, Kamathipura, opened in areas where Chinese families settled in the late 19th century.

18 This swell in population is explained by the presence of Chinese soldiers during the Second World War, many in Calcutta, who were sent to India by the then ruling Chinese (Kuomintang) government of Chiang Kai-shek,

to fight alongside Allied soldiers on India's eastern front against Japanese forces. Many stayed behind with the establishment of the People's Republic of China on 1 October 1949.

19 The Meiji Restoration (1868) is a reference to the restoration of powers back to the Imperial Japanese Emperor, after more than two and a half centuries (1603 to 1867) of dominance by military dictators known as the Tokugawa Shoguns. Imperial Japan under the Shoguns had chosen national seclusion from the rest of the world and only permitted Dutch and Chinese merchants to trade through its southern port of Nagasaki. In 1858, with a much weakened Shogunate in charge, the western powers, led by the United States, were demanding access to Japanese ports and markets, which resulted in Japan signing its first Treaty of Amity and Commerce (the Harris Treaty signed with the United States on 29 July 1858). This opened the ports of Nagasaki, Yokohama and Shimoda to foreign traders that year.

20 This information is taken from the average membership numbers of the Mumbai Japanese Association, a group made up of Japanese nationals and those who may have a Japanese spouse.

21 What differentiated the *Karayuki San* from Japanese workers in India and elsewhere was that they mostly originated from the impoverished Anakusa Islands of western Kyushu, a small region, while Japanese workers came from all over Japan.

22 The Japanese cemetery in Mumbai is possibly the only one belonging to the community in India. This is indicative of the city's age-old ties through trade with Japan. It once possessed a structure atop which a funeral pyre could be built. It also has two *stambhas* (columns) of which the older of the two is the buff-coloured one.

23 One should not confuse the current Mitsui & Co. Ltd. India, as being a continuation of the old one. They are two separate corporate entities.

24 Nippon Menkwa Kabushiki Kaisha was headquartered in Osaka. The Bombay office was located in Nippon Building on Outram Road.

25 The Tommen and Nichimen firms by 1918–1919 had a mix of Japanese and Indian employees who went into the cotton growing regions to buy and have the raw cotton ginned (cleaned) and baled, and then transported to the city for shipping to Japan. It appears that these two firms conducted the inland purchases for the Japanese firms in Bombay.

Bibliography

Aroon, Tikekar. 1994. *A Century of Ties: Bombay and Japan*. Bombay: The Consulate General of Japan in Bombay.

1865. *Bombay Almanac and Directory*. Bombay: Bombay Gazette Press.

Caroe, Olaf. 1958. *The Pathans, 550 B.C.–A.D. 1957*. New York: St. Martin's Press.

Durazi, I. and Daruwala, S, interview by Lentin Sifra. 2019. History of Irani Masjid and Community (June 13).

Edwardes, Stephen Meredyth. 1909. *The Gazetteer of Bombay City and Island*. Reprint 1977. Vol. 1. 3 vols. Bombay, Bombay: Gazetteer Department.

Encyclopaedia Britannica. n.d. *'Early Republican Period' and 'Late Republican Period' in Introduction & Quick Facts: China.* Accessed October 29, 2017. https://www.britannica.com/place/China/Cultural-institutions#toc214398.

Harald, Fisher-Tine. 2003. "White Women Degrading Themselves to the Lowest Depths: European Networks of Prostitution." *The Indian Economic and Social History Review (Sage)* 40 (2): 177.

Hsieh, Ming Tung, interview by Lentin. 2017. *Chinese Community in India.*

Jackson, Stanley. 1968. *The Sassoons.* London: William Heinemann.

Jalali Sayed, Namazi Ali, interview by Lentin Sifra. 2019. *History of Irani Masjid and Community* (June 13).

Ling, interview by Lentin. 2017. *Chinese restaurants in Bombay*

n.d. "Living with Gandhi: Rev. Fujii Guruji in India and the Indo-Japanese Relations in the 1930s."

Mohiuddin, M., and Poonawala I. K. 2009. 'Bombay: Persian Muslim Communities', in E. Yarshater (ed.), *Encylopaedia Iranica.* New York: Bibliotheca Persica Press. Accessed on 30 May 2019.

Nile, Green. 2011. *Bombay Islam.* New Delhi: Cambridge University Press.

Nishumura, Suzuki Michie. 2012. *The Origins of International Banking in Asia.* UK: OUP.

Overy, Richard. 2011. *The Times Complete History of the World.* London: Harper Collins.

n.d. *Political Residency Bushire.* Accessed August 13, 2019. https://www.qdl.qa/en/political-residency-bushire.

Rachel, Manasseh. 2013. *Baghdadian Jews of Bombay: Their Life & Achievements, A Personal And Historical Account.* New York: Midrash BEN ISH HAI.

Ramakrishna, Chatterjee. 2010. "The Chinese Community in Calcutta." In *India and China in the Colonial World*, by Thampi Madhavi Ed., 61–62. New Delhi: Social Science Press.

Rao, Deepak, interview by Lentin Sifra. 2019. *Pathans in Bombay.*

Roland, Joan. 1998. *Jews in British India: Identity in a Colonial Era.* New Brunswick, N.J.: Transaction Publishers.

San, Bhikshu Morita, interview by Sifra Lentin. 2019. *Japanese Temple* (February 9).

Sarwari, interview by Lentin. 2019. *Afghanistan's trade with India.*

Tham, interview by Lentin. 2018. *Chinese community in Bombay.*

Tung, Hsieh Ming. 2012. *India's Chinese A Lost Tribe.* Kolkata: Self.

Yapp, M.E. 1967. "The Establishment of the East India Company Residency at Baghdad, 1798–1806." *Bulletin of the School of Oriental and Arican Studies* 30 (Fiftieth Anniversary Volume): 323–336.

Yasmin, Khan. 2015. *The Raj At War: A People's History of India's Second World War.* Gurgaon: Random House Publishers.

5 Finance, *desi* and *videshi*

The rise of Bombay as a global center for money and credit during the 19th and early half of the 20th centuries can be broadly correlated to the decline of Surat – the Mughal port city, whose rise to prominence began under the rule of the Mughal Emperor Akbar (r. 1556–1605). Surat's trading communities – both local and foreign – and indigenous bankers, slowly relocated to Bombay or opened branches here (detailed in Chapters 3 and 4), bringing with them their local and overseas trading and credit networks.

By 1869, when the Suez Canal opened, Bombay city was at its apogee, and considered the most important city 'east of Suez'. This was a time when cities like Shanghai, Hong Kong, Singapore and Yokohama, which were to become Bombay's contemporaries in the early 20th century, were still in their infancy. It was during the cotton boom of 1861–1865 that the merchandise exports of Bombay Presidency (headquartered in the city) peaked, and it had overtaken – for the first time – Bengal Presidency in terms of external trade revenue. In the peak years of 1864 and 1865, Bombay's exports at £37,291,186 and £39,385,822, respectively, were double that of Bengal's exports of £18,640,221 and £17,759,476 for these years (Bagchi 2007).[1]

Colonial Bombay has never been written about as a global financial hub, but recent writings by urban historians (Ghadge, 2018) have begun reframing it as such. This is particularly relevant for the period beginning 1870 till the Second World War, when the city was deeply integrated into the global economy. Rediscovering this period of the city's financial history can be revelatory because of the financial fluencies between this past and its present in the 21st century, when the very same foreign banks, insurance companies and credit networks of this period are re-establishing themselves in Mumbai today.

Bombay's historic connections overseas through the Indian rupee (a multilateral currency); the co-opting of its indigenous banking

DOI: 10.4324/9781003182894-5

network by the EEIC and Agency Houses to facilitate their foreign trade; foreign banks, eastern exchange banks (or British Overseas Banks), and, after 1935, India's central bank, are some aspects of its financial ecosystem, networks and overseas connections that made Bombay the most important city in the east. As detailed in Chapters 1 and 2, a large part of the city's overseas influence is attributable to its port and the vast hinterland it controlled after the Maratha and Mysore wars, making Bombay a commercial and financial node.

Admittedly, the economic interests of British India were always subservient to that of the United Kingdom, as expressed most succinctly in Dadabhai Naoroji's 'drain theory', but contemporary studies of Indian merchants on the subcontinent's west coast and their indigenous banking system – powered by the *Hundi,* a most versatile financial instrument – demonstrate that more often than not, the big bankers and merchants (including the British Agency Houses) often called the shots here, unlike in Calcutta, the capital city of British India till 1911. They financed, underwrote and insured every exportable commodity – like cotton, indigo, opium – from the moment they were sown in the field, to harvesting, packing, transport to port cities and their export overseas. Local merchants not only dominated the Indian Ocean trade but popularised the usage of the Indian rupee in their vast overseas networks. It was only in 17th-and 18th-century trade with Great Britain that the Company and the English Agency Houses enjoyed a monopoly.

Therefore, this chapter attempts to contextualise some aspects of Bombay the international financial city, albeit a colonial one, in the regional and global economy. The first step was taken with the EEIC insinuating itself into local credit networks and later that of their currency – the Bombay rupee (as also the Bengal *Sicca* and Madras Arcot rupee) – into the Indian Ocean maritime world. The rupee established not just the political authority of the Company but helped secure its success as a trading firm.

The Bombay rupee

This began when the Company at Bombay received Royal Letters Patent (15 October 1676) empowering it to mint its own coins (Edwardes 1909), the terms were clear – it was 'to be called rupees, *pices* and *bujruks* or any other names the Company might adopt provided they were not the names of any coins current in the Kings dominions'.

The first silver rupee of the EEIC struck at the Bombay Mint in March 1677, bore the royal coat of arms and the legend 'By authority of Charles II' and stamped 'Rupee of Bombaim'. It was established to the silver standard then prevalent in the Mughal Empire. This silver standard of 1 *tola* (about 11.6 gm) weight originated during the reign of Iltutmish (1211–1236), the third ruler of the Mamluk (slave) dynasty of Delhi. It was standardised by the currency reforms of Sher Shah Suri about 1538–1539 who also gave the denomination its name 'rūpyam' (silver coin; Bhandare 2007).

Under the Mughals, the rupee became a pan-Indian coin with mints spread from Balkh (in present day Uzbekistan) in the north to Trichinpalli (in the present state of Tamil Nadu) in the south. The decline of the Mughal Empire after the death of Aurangzeb in 1707 resulted in monetary disarray and the rupee was once again standardised in 1835 to a coin of 1 *tola* weight (11.66 gm) of 11/12th (0.917) fine silver. Variations of the *tola* weight standard thus remained in vogue till 1940 – over a period of 500 years (Shaikh 2013).

The early coins struck by the Company in European style did not circulate widely. The Portuguese and other land powers like the Marathas resisted accepting coins from the Bombay mint as this would acknowledge the political authority of the Company. On the islands themselves, locals preferred to use the Portuguese *Xeraphins* and *Reas.* For trade purposes, however, they needed to be converted into rupees at the Mughal mint typically at Surat for acceptability.

In 1717, the EEIC acquired the right to mint coins in the Mughal idiom under Emperor Farrukhsiyar's policy of outsourcing mints to private entities. These Mughal style coins with Persian inscriptions facilitated their acceptance in trade and for common usage.

Therefore, the Bombay rupee succeeded because it piggybacked on the widespread usage of the Mughal silver (Surat) rupee – its prototype. It was interchangeably known as a 'Surat'. Like the Surat rupee, its uniformity, purity and weight, which corresponded to about half the value of the Spanish peso or eight-real piece (minted in the Latin Americas) and the Maria Theresa Thaler (a silver bullion coin first minted in 1741), both popular trading currencies, ensured the rupee fit neatly into the monetary mechanism of the East Indies trade.

The monetary disarray that followed the breakup of the Mughal Empire led to the emergence of a number of currencies **issued by** native states. This in turn gave rise to a thriving *shroff* (money-changer) community in Bombay. The *shroffs* charged a commission on the exchange of and for assaying (determining the metallic purity) different coins whether for purposes of internal or overseas trade. What existed then was a multi-lateral currency regime in the Indian Ocean trading world, where the circulation and intrinsic value of a currency depended on the weight and purity of the metal used. This made the Surat mint, which coined the Surat rupee, the most productive mint in the Mughal empire. This was the reason why the Bombay coins were minted to the Surat standard.

Over time three different currencies emerged in British India for minting the silver rupee. Company coins minted in Bengal were known as the *Sicca;* in Madras, they were known as the Arcot rupee, and in Bombay, they were called the Surat rupee. Names that were indicative of the prototype they were based on. By 1800, Surat came to be administered by the Company's government in Bombay, and by October 1815, the Surat mint was closed. Therefore, the Bombay mint supplied the entire coinage of Bombay Presidency, and its coins were interchangeably referred to as Surat rupees (Edwardes 1909). By then, the British Indian rupee had already made inroads into overseas trading and credit networks by piggybacking on the Mughal rupee.

The rupee a globally traded currency

In the littoral regions of the Arabian Sea, the rupee pre-dated the European companies – it was accepted and used by the centuries-old trading networks between the Indian subcontinent and the ports of the Persian Gulf, the Arabian Sea and the Red Sea. It was a popular currency circulating in multilateral currency markets, like the annual Haj. Moreover, age-old Indian trading diasporas in West Asia, like in Muscat & Oman and Omani-ruled Zanzibar, preferred using the rupee and its denominations because of their trade with the west coast of India. Often the rupee was introduced into usage among host populations by the Indian overseas diaspora, like in the case of East Africa.

In the case of Muscat & Oman, the Bombay silver rupee, the copper quarter anna and the 12 anna coins (the latter two known as the *baisa* and *ghazi*, respectively), were all naturalised as Omani currency by being countermarked by this sheikhdom, as were other popular currencies. The Bombay rupee, and later the British Indian rupee, became the de facto circulating currency in this region and Omani-ruled Zanzibar when they came under the British sphere of influence, which began with the signing of the anti-slavery treaties from 1803 to 1873. Various factors contributed to the rupee's growing legitimacy, including the establishment of a British consular court in Zanzibar to settle trade disputes – with appeals being heard in the High Court in Bombay – and the important and growing presence of Indian merchant communities from the Presidency of Bombay there.

The history of the rupee in the Trucial (Treaty) states (present-day UAE – i.e. Dubai, Abu Dhabi, Ras al-Khaimah, Ajman, Sharjah, Fujairah and Umm al-Quwain) was slightly different. Unlike Oman, these states were notorious for piracy on British flagged ships. In fact, the first large anti-piracy expedition of 1805 to this region was sent from Bombay, but piracy kept reappearing in the Gulf. Eventually, the Company at Bombay decided to establish a police force in the region to keep piracy in check. This administrative intervention, consisting of British and Indian manpower – who were paid in Bombay rupees – contributed greatly to the local usage of the rupee here.

Subsequently, the Indian rupee became legal tender in the Trucial coast when each of the seven sheikhdoms signed a treaty with Great Britain that was fiduciary in nature and bound them together into a loose confederate. It was the 1892 maritime treaty, which earned them the name Trucial (Treaty) States. It was alternatively known as the 'exclusion' treaty or exclusive agreement, as it was used by the British to keep out growing Russian and French influence in the region. Under the financial clauses of this treaty, the fiscal administration of these states was linked to the British Indian government. It was this that made the British Indian rupee official legal tender here, and later led to these states maintaining a sterling reserve with the RBI, after its establishment in 1935, in lieu of the rupees issued to them. This fiscal administration by the RBI continued well after Indian independence too. The demonetisation of the Indian rupee by 1970 by these countries – the last being Oman – has ensured living memories of the rupee as a local Gulf currency.

Other overseas regions where the Indian rupee circulated as the de facto and de jure currency were regions that became part of British India – like Burma (today's Myanmar) – or those that came under direct British rule, like Ceylon (Sri Lanka) (Shaikh, The Conjuror's Trick: An Interpretive History of Paper Money in India 2020).

Another region where the British Indian rupee became the official currency for a brief period was the British East Africa Protectorate, which consisted of the territories of the Imperial British East Africa Company (IBEAC) – which had colonised the Mrima Coast and Kenya, Zanzibar (it became a British protectorate in 1890) and the kingdom of Buganda (Uganda). The Indian rupee was already a popular currency in East Africa in the 19th century, as the small monetised segment of its population were largely dominated by Indian, Swahili and Arab traders.

In the British Protectorate of East Africa, before the East African Currency Board (London) was set up in 1919 for the stated purpose of introducing a British colonial currency not linked to the silver rupee of British India, the rupee was a popular circulating currency (not official) among a pool of currencies. Problems arose in 1916 during the First World War, when the intrinsic value of the rupee exceeded its par value because of the phenomenal rise in the global price of silver. The silver Indian rupee had to be revaluated higher based on its silver content to two shillings four deuce from its pre-war value of one shilling four deuce to the sterling pound. Unfortunately, the Protectorate's currency reserves were stored in sterling pounds, which had devalued vis-à-vis the circulating rupee. British India's silver reserves too were at an all-time high, although the Indian rupee itself was on a flexible gold exchange standard then.[2] This crisis marked the exit of the rupee from East Africa, with the introduction of its own currency.

The Indian rupee had a longer run in the Gulf states, persisting as the official currency even after Indian independence in 1947. India's RBI managed the fiscal administration of what is today's UAE, Bahrain, Qatar and Oman well into the late 1960s. What impelled these countries to shift to their own currency was the deteriorating foreign exchange situation in India and the possibilities of misuse of this arrangement especially for gold trafficking. To obviate such possibilities, special Gulf Rupee notes were issued in 1959 for circulation exclusively outside India. The impending devaluation of the Indian rupee and nascent nationalism prompted these countries to issue their own currencies bringing to an end the circulation of the Indian rupee as a global traded currency.

An attempt was made in the 1960s to conduct rupee-based trade with the Soviet bloc countries in order to save precious foreign exchange. This turned out to be a flawed model – and was abandoned by the 1980s – largely because Indian goods sold to these countries were often routed into the West using switch-trading. This effectively deprived India of precious foreign exchange earnings (Batliwalla 1998).

The *Hundi:* oiling the wheels of trade and war

Much before the establishment of Anglo-Saxon banking in Bombay, it was the indigenous banking system, popularly known as the *Hundi* system – named after its versatile credit instrument the *Hundi* – which could (depending on its purpose) double up as a bill of exchange, a promissory note, letter of credit or remittance vehicle – that took care of local, coastal and pan-Asian trade (Martin 2009).

Though the city did get its first modern bank in 1720, it appears to have played a limited role in Bombay's financial ecosystem being more a savings bank set up for the Company's employees by the EEIC government in Bombay Castle. It functioned till 1778 before going into oblivion. There was no demand for another bank for the city till the 1830s, because Bombay already had a strong informal (*Hundi*) banking sector. One indication of this is a reference to a large community of indigenous bankers functioning almost parallel to the first English bank in Bombay, indicating that the native network for the transfer and creation of credit, particularly within the subcontinent, West Asia and East Africa, had existed for at least a few hundred years. In 1753, some big and established bankers from Aurangabad and Poona opened business on the Island. They were attracted to the city, as it had become the centre of trade between western and upper India, and between the Malabar Coast, the Persian Gulf and the Red Sea.

By the 19th century, banking in the city was in the hands of about a hundred Hindu *shroffs* (indigenous bankers), whose business premises were largely in Bazaar Gate Street, and whose bills and *hundis* (promissory notes) were accepted and honoured in all parts of India (Edwardes 1909). Some large *shroffs* had offices in all other major cities like Calcutta, Madras, Karachi, Hyderabad and Surat. Although the reference is to Hindu *shroffs*, it is pertinent to note that most big 19th century Bombay merchants also acted as indigenous bankers. One notable example is David Sassoon whose home and office on 9, Tamarind Lane (Fort) would be frequented by Afghan caravan traders and captains of *dhows* who largely plied the Basra–Baghdad route, where Sassoon had his contacts. Most were outside the pale of British mercantile law but were using the traditional trans-Asian and Indian Ocean credit networks. Here they would take loans against unsold merchandise, entrust their earnings for safe-keeping, draw up bills of exchange and promissory notes, exchange currency and in general transact all banking business (Jackson 1968).

The indigenous banker (different from the local moneylender) covered a wide spectrum of banking activities: financing wholesale and retail trade; accepting deposits; giving loans to individuals, firms and the EEIC; handling remittances, discounting bills of exchange, mint masters and money changers; and collecting revenue for the government. In the 19th and early 20th centuries, they were the main source of credit for trade and industry in the city (Chandavarkar 2013). It was only the foreign exchange business that the native banking sector did not cover. International remittances and discounting of sterling denominated bills of exchange in London were the exclusive purview of the English Agency Houses, the East India Company and by the mid-19th century, of the British overseas banks (or eastern exchange banks) and the branch offices of foreign banks.

This foreign exchange business proved critical to the profits of Bombay merchants involved in the Bombay–Canton trade. It was the scarcity of good bills drawn on the Supreme Government at Calcutta, and on the Court of Directors at London, that was a major obstacle faced by Bombay's China traders in remitting funds to India after the First Opium War (Siddiqi 1982). This was one of the key factors that led to a consolidation in the China trade, resulting only in big merchants – like the Bombay headquartered Sassoon and Tata families who opened branches in London, Hong Kong, Shanghai, Yokohama – participating in this trade, with numerous small traders and investors pulling out.

What is noteworthy is that in spite of the EEIC monopoly on trade with India till 1813 and that of China till 1833, there always existed a high degree of interdependence between local bankers, merchants, Agency Houses and the Company in Bombay in order to facilitate overseas trade. This was particularly highlighted in times of war and during monetary crisis, often resulting in the bailing out of the Company by the indigenous banking network.

Modern banking in the city: reasons for a delayed beginning

In 1835, a second attempt was made to establish a bank in the city when a Government Savings Bank was established at Bombay Castle, for the convenience of the Company's employees. This gap of 57 years from the closure of the first to the establishment of a second bank in Bombay probably indicates the effective handling of the cash and credit needs of the city by indigenous bankers, Agency Houses and the Company's treasury.

In the same year (1835), when a uniform rupee coinage was introduced in all the Company's territories on the subcontinent, 2,000 indigenous bankers from Bombay petitioned the government that they would be deprived of their highly lucrative commission charges on the exchange of money (Chandavarkar, Kumar & Raychaudhuri , 2013). The large number of petitioners against uniform coinage of the rupee indicates the size of the native banking sector in the early 19th century. However, business historian Amiya Bagchi points to political reasons for the late beginnings of a modern bank for Bombay (Bagchi, The Evolution of the State Bank of India: The Roots 1806–1876 1987).

For one, the city was not politically and financially stable. Unlike Calcutta, Bombay did not have a hinterland that it politically controlled in the late 18th century, though it had become a significant port for the export of cotton (and later opium) to China, and had extensive trade with West Asia and East Africa. But the natural hinterland of the city that produced these raw materials were part of native kingdoms. This gave the Company little control over the price, quality and quantity of raw products (cotton, opium) as well as manufactured products (cotton piece goods). It had to depend on local merchants and the Agency Houses with their native networks to procure these goods for the Company to ship to China. Moreover, a monopoly could not be established in Bombay, as the Company had done with indigo and opium in Bengal Presidency.

Expensive wars with the Marathas further compounded this situation; they bankrupted the Bombay government to such an extent that at one point there was a move to reduce its status from a Presidency to just a factory (a trading establishment at a foreign port) in the late 18th century (Nightingale Reprint 2008). During the Anglo-Maratha Wars (1792–1819), the solvency of Bombay depended on the Presidency of Bengal, funds transferred from the Presidency of Bengal via *hundi* through the big native bankers like Arunji Nathji, loans from big Agency Houses like Forbes & Co. and Bruce, Fawcett & Co. and from big local merchants, kept the Presidency of Bombay solvent. In just 16 years from 1792–1793 to 1808–1809, Bombay's excess of expenditure over revenues amounted to £ 18,385,745 (Bagchi, The Evolution of the State Bank of India: The Roots 1806–1876 1987).

A loan taken by the Bombay government on 1 December 1801 exemplifies the nexus between the Company's merchants, the Agency Houses and big local merchants, who virtually directed the financial affairs of the Company in Bombay during the ruinous Maratha Wars. This was one of many loans raised by the government locally, when it sold its entire stock of 85,000 bales of cotton at the cost price of Rs 10 per bale to seven Bombay merchants – a mix of Company servants, and private European and native merchants. Among the Europeans were Charles Forbes, founder of the Agency House of Forbes & Co.; Henry Fawcett, a junior merchant of the East India Company, accountant general of the Bombay government, and partner of the Agency House of Bruce, Fawcett & Company; and Alexander Adamson, a junior merchant of the Company, who held the post of assistant to the treasurer, and a founder of the Agency House of Scott, Tate & Adamson (Nightingale Reprint 2008). Among the local merchants were Hormusjee Bomanjee and Pestonjee (Wadia brothers), Ardasheer Dadyshet and Sorabjee Muncherjee Readymoney. Company servants in Bombay, unlike in Calcutta, were allowed private trade till 1806. As a result, they often placed their personal interests above that of the Company. This practice was finally ended in 1806 (Bagchi, The Evolution of the State Bank of India: The Roots 1806–1876 1987).

'But the power of the private traders in Bombay', as Historian Pamela Nightingale succinctly put it in her book *Trade And Empire In Western India 1784–1806*, 'did not rest solely on their role as bankers to the government. Throughout most of the 18th century the private traders in Bombay were the government' (Nightingale Reprint 2008). This led to big merchants using the Company's treasury at Bombay as their own private bank of deposit, an important reason why Bombay got its first chartered, modern bank much later than Calcutta.

Besides, all functions of an exchange bank in financing foreign trade were undertaken by the EEIC and the Agency Houses. It was only after 1851, when the first British overseas bank – Oriental Bank Corporation – was permitted to enter the foreign exchange business that the role of the EEIC and the Agency Houses began waning (Suzuki, et al. 2012). Indigenous bankers did not do this, because it required a tie-up with a London 'correspondent bank' that was plugged into the London inter-bank money market. British overseas banks, being headquartered in London, with branches in the East, had no such restrictions. In fact, they pioneered the development of international banking by following the model established by the East India Company (Suzuki, et al. 2012).

The times were propitious too, as from the 1870s till 1914, the first global economy began coalescing, where the ancient Indian Ocean trading world was further integrated with an industrialising Atlantic world, through communications (telegraph, the opening of the Suez and Panama canals) and through international banking, currency and commodity markets (Overy 2010). An important financial instrument to transfer and create credit, and facilitate remittances during this period, was the sterling denominated bills of exchange on London, which were issued against bills of lading (both exports and imports). London's bill discounting market facilitated by bill brokers was key to creating liquidity for banks who bought these bills from traders.

Pertinently, when the chartered presidency Bank of Bombay was founded in 1840, it was the foreign exchange business that was precluded from its charter because of it being too risky. For remittances, however, most Company employees still preferred to send their funds via private business channels, like private European merchants, American merchants and Agency Houses, rather than through the official channels of the EEIC. This was for an obvious reason: their earnings on the subcontinent were far in excess of their salaries even *after* private trade was forbidden in Bombay in 1806. This made private investments in the China trade, in the businesses of Agency Houses and private English and American merchants, a more attractive option.

Old Bank of Bombay (1840) and Bank of Western India (1842)

The establishment of the Bank of Bombay in 1840, a quasi-government, chartered, presidency entity, marked the beginning of modern banking in the city. The Bank of Bombay was the second of the three chartered presidency banks established in the subcontinent then, along with the Bank of Bengal (1806/1809) and the Bank of Madras (1843). A chartered bank was different from other forms of banks at the time – both indigenous banking establishments and joint stock banks. The acquisition of a charter issued either by the Court of Directors of the EEIC or the Privy Council insulated the bank from unlimited liability. This meant that in the event of the bank's failure, the liability of its shareholders would be limited to the face value or a multiple of their share-holding.

As explained earlier, the Company, the Agency Houses and the city's big merchants resisted the opening of a bank in Bombay. It was the opening of the India trade in 1813 that brought in a whole tier of second-level players and private merchants, who began to clamour for a presidency bank for Bombay on the same lines as that of the Presidency Bank of Bengal. The Scottish trader John Skinner (of Skinner & Co.), one of the founders of the Bombay Chamber of Commerce (est.1833), chaired a meeting on 26 December 1836 to garner public support to establish a chartered presidency bank for Bombay.

It is noteworthy that just two days *before* this first meeting, a memorial against the setting up of the bank was presented by the city's established Agency Houses and big merchants to the government. It stated that 'no advantage would flow from the establishment of a bank, while numerous evils would arise from an issue of currency notes, which did not represent real capital' (Bagchi, The Evolution of the State Bank of India: The Roots 1806–1876 1987). The reference is to paper currency issue, which was then one of the functions of a bank. This power to issue currency was taken away later under the Paper Currency Act (1861), and transferred to a government administered Paper Currency Department. The period prior to 1861 when banks in India issued their own bank notes is also known as the period of free banking (Shaikh, The Conjuror's Trick: An Interpretive History of Paper Money in India 2020).

The Bank of Bombay was founded four years later (April 1840), marking the beginning of the first Anglo-Saxon, joint-stock, banking institution in the city. Foreign exchange banking was the only function this bank was precluded to do by its Charter, as were the other two presidency banks. The three chartered banks even after their merger and reconstitution as the Imperial Bank of India in 1921 could not directly participate in the London money market. In the early years after their merger it was restricted to borrowing and lending through 'correspondents' in London, for periods not exceeding six months (before 1907, it was three months)[3] (Chandavarkar 2013). Eventually the Imperial Bank of India Act (1934) lifted the restriction to directly engage in the forex business, which put this Bank (renamed State Bank of India in 1955) finally on par with the many British overseas banks and branches of foreign banks that were operating in the city at this time.

It was in order to overcome this hurdle of access to foreign exchange banking by smaller merchants, that just two years after the Bank of Bombay was established, another bank was set up in the city – Bank of Western India. This Bombay bank – due to the hurdles it faced in acquiring a Charter – by a twist of fate became the first British overseas bank after it finally shifted headquarters to London. Following its example some Bombay banks shifted headquarters to London, or specialised eastern exchange banks opened in London with branches in India, or foreign banks from other countries, entered the forex business in Bombay and India.

The stated objective of the Bank of Western India was to enter the exchange banking business. This was intended to break the entry barrier for merchants from Britain and Europe, who had to pay heavy agency commissions to the EEIC and established Agency Houses, to begin trade with Bombay. The Bank of Western India was founded in 1842, with a share capital of Rs. 80 lakh. Originally headquartered in the city, it had to later shift to a structure of dual head offices – Bombay and London – till it finally shifted its head office to London, and constituted an all-European board. This Bank's original promoters, like those of the Bank of Bombay, were a mix of Europeans and Indians, who had got together to break the EEIC and Agency House monopoly on foreign trade with India. Most notable among the local businessmen were Sir Jaganath (Nana) Shankarsett and Framjee Cowasjee.

The Bank of Western India was a trailblazer for global banking in Bombay for three reasons. It was the first British overseas bank or eastern exchange bank. Second, its quest for a charter that would include forex banking – a nine-year-long litigious journey – created the prototype and led to the establishment of many new British overseas banks. Lastly, foreign banks specialising in the trade between India and their home country – like the Yokohama Specie Bank – also set up operations in India *after* the Oriental Bank Corporation (formerly Bank of Western India) acquired its charter on 30 August 1851. The last bastion – forex banking – of the EEIC and established Agency Houses had been finally breached.

The Oriental Bank Corporation went on to become the largest and most profitable exchange bank in the world in the 19th century. It had branches and agencies across the world, except for North and South America. Before the acquisition of its charter, some of its branches in addition to Bombay were Calcutta, Madras, Colombo, Kandy, Mauritius, Singapore, Hong Kong, Canton, Shanghai, Sydney, Melbourne and London (Suzuki, et al. 2012). It issued its own currency notes, which circulated alongside those of the Bank of Bombay. Moreover, in its desperation to acquire a charter, it bought over the chartered Bank of Ceylon in 1849 (Jisc Archives Hub n.d.). The Charter it finally obtained in 1851 enabled its entry into the London forex market and empowered it to undertake exchange, deposit and remittance business anywhere to the East of the Cape of Good Hope. It's currency notes also circulated in Ceylon, Hong Kong and other parts of China and South East Asia, making it Bombay's first truly international bank.

As the following table shows, on every criterion this bank was the largest and the most successful eastern exchange bank of its time (Table 5.1).

Table 5.1 Major eastern exchange banks (as on 31 December 1877, in £)

Banks	Paid-up capital	Reserve + dividend + undivided profit	Deposit	Dividend %
Oriental Bank Corporation	1,500,000	408,423	11,999,407	10
HSBC	1,000,000	240,617	4,063,423	7 1/8
Chartered Bank of India, Australia & China (CBIAC)	800,000	180,311	2,383,834	6
Chartered Mercantile Bank	750,000	181,561	3,778,126	8
National Bank of India	935,500	38,442	1,523,638	6

Source: *The Economist*, 18 May 1878, pp. 6–7 (Suzuki, et al. 2012).
Note: HK$1 = 4 shillings (£1= HK $ 5).

International banking in Bombay

With the Oriental Bank creating the prototype for an eastern exchange bank, three types of foreign exchange banks opened for business in India.

Banks which over time became sterling denominated British overseas (or eastern exchange) banks that were headquartered in London. These early British overseas banks that opened for business in the city were the Commercial Bank of India (Bombay, 1845) and Mercantile Bank of India, London and China Ltd (Bombay, 1854), both subsequently shifted their head office to London in 1857; the Chartered Bank of India, Australia & China (London, 1858) and National Bank of India Ltd. (London, 1863) opened in London. Another such bank, but with headquarters in Hong Kong, was the Hong Kong and Shanghai Banking Corporation (HSBC), which opened its Bombay branch in 1869. Out of these 19th-century banks, HSBC and Standard Chartered Bank – formed by a merger of the city's early British overseas bank Chartered Bank of India, Australia & China and Standard Bank of British South Africa, in 1969 – have continuously operated in the city.

In the second category were foreign banks that specialised in trade between their respective countries and India. Among the earliest foreign banks to open branches in the city were the *Comptoir National D' Escompte* (Paris) in 1861, the Yokohama Specie Bank Ltd. (Yokohama, Japan) in 1894, and the New York headquartered International Banking Corporation in 1904 (Bagchi, The Evolution of the State Bank of India: The Roots 1806–1876 1987). The Yokohama Specie Bank in particular, used its London office as a pivot to manage the triangular trade between Bombay, Yokohama and the United States.

Lastly, among the Indian joint stock banks that established branches in London and transacted a limited amount of exchange business was the Bombay-based Indian Specie Bank (which financed trade in pearls and specie). It failed in 1929 due to speculation in silver. In this category was also the Tata Industrial Bank (that amalgamated in August 1923 with the Central Bank of India), and the Alliance Bank of Simla, which was liquidated in 1923 (Dadabhoy 2013). Another Indian exchange bank to open in London was the Central Exchange Bank of India (a subsidiary of the Central Bank of India) in 1936; just two years later, it merged with Barclays Bank (London).

The restriction on the Imperial Bank of India (an amalgamated entity comprising the three presidency banks) to engage in the foreign exchange business was removed on the recommendation of the Central Banking

Enquiry Committee (1929–1931). It was this same Committee – popularly known as the Hilton Young Committee – that recommended that a separate Reserve Bank of India be set up rather than changing the status of the Imperial Bank of India to a central bank.

The case for a central bank for India: stabilising the rupee

But central banking policy for British-administered India remained under the control of various bodies headquartered in London. One of London's main preoccupations was the exchange value of the Indian rupee vis á vis the British sterling pound – this was important in order to maintain a favourable balance of trade for England.

Initially, it was the Company's court of directors that handled this key function. Later, it was done by the Board of Control (1784–1858), the India Office, and finally by the finance committee (that assisted the Secretary of State for India) in consultation with the finance member of the viceroy's council.

Often, the currency ratios between the British pound and the Indian rupee were a matter of fierce debate between the Indian mercantile community and the various currency commissions that were sent to India between the years 1866–1925. During these currency debates, the recommendation for a central bank for India to look to the interests of India was often brought up.

Interestingly, some post-colonial histories on central banking in India suggest that the preoccupation of the Indian mercantile community and the India Office with the exchange value of the Indian rupee vis á vis the sterling pound actually took the focus away from the need to establish a central bank for India – a recommendation of the currency commissions, particularly the Royal Commission (Chamberlain) on Indian Finance and Currency (1910).

The wildly fluctuating rupee was caused by the different currency standards, the subcontinent was first on silver and after 1898, the gold exchange standard, as against Britain that was on the gold standard. The irascibility of the rupee was caused more by the global fluctuations in the price of silver combined with it being a highly regulated currency.

An obvious solution was establishing a central bank on the subcontinent that would take independent monetary decisions in the interest of India. But this would mean a potential power centre and rival to the Bank of England (founded in 1694) and the British Treasury. Still there were some personalities within the British establishment, who genuinely cared about the negative fall-out of not having a central bank, like British economist John Maynard Keynes, who consistently championed the cause of a central bank for India in the early 20th century (Chandavarkar 2013).

The Royal Commission on Indian Currency and Finance, 1927 (Hilton-Young Commission) recommended the establishment of a central bank to be called the Reserve Bank of India as a shareholders' bank. The Reserve Bank of India Bill 1927 however had to be dropped in view of irreconcilable differences on governance matters. The first central bank to be set up in a British colony was the Central Bank of South Africa in 1929. Six years later, the RBI was finally established on 1 April 1935, as a private joint stock bank.

According to former International Monetary Fund (IMF) Economist Anand G. Chandavarkar's chapter 'Money and Credit (1858–1947)' in the *Cambridge Economic History of India*, when the RBI initially began functioning, it did not undertake many of the roles that we identify with it today. He writes,

> The effects of the delayed establishment of the RBI should not be exaggerated, more particularly because in an underdeveloped economy, a central bank, at least in its initial phases, has distinctly limited potentialities for monetary control...For instance, the RBI was unable to activate the 'bank rate technique' until about 1951.

The establishment of the RBI could not have been more timely and its effect stabilising, as it was established when the Indian nationalistic movement had gained momentum in the inter-war years, and soon after the global economy was beset with the Great Depression (1928). Most importantly, it played a critical role in protecting the country's interests during the Bretton Woods conference (1944) in the United States, at a time when Indian independence was inevitable after the War. It was the only British colony that had its own representatives.

The Indian delegation succeeded in securing India's large sterling balance of Rs. 1,736 crore (1940–1946) with the Bank of England against the expected devaluation after the Second World War of the British sterling pound. India's contribution to the Second World War was not just the largest from among the British colonies, but it was made at great personal sacrifice – it exported food grains – at a time when the country was beset by the terrible Bengal famine (1943–1944). This sterling balance represented this sacrifice! Devaluation would mean wiping out a substantial part of India's reimbursable war reserves with Britain. Although, the RBI delegation did not succeed in securing multi-lateral convertibility of India's sterling reserves with the Bank of England into US dollars, the assurance given by Lord John

Maynard Keynes at Bretton Woods, the moving spirit of the conference and head of the British delegation, was that a suitable bilateral
arrangement would be worked out – and it was.

India bid then too – unsuccessfully – for a permanent (not elected)
seat on the Executive Board of the IMF and World Bank, on the basis
of its anticipated post-war trade. In 2016 following reforms passed in
2010, India's IMF Quota (also calculated as Special Drawing Rights or
SDR's) was increased to 2.66% from 2.44% making it the eighth-largest
Quota country but still not among the top five (IMF n.d.). The greater
the Quota the greater the voting rights in this Fund. The 16th General
Review of Quotas which will be concluded by 15 December 2023 should
result in an increase in India's Quota (and heft), given the country's
large GDP and forex reserves in spite of a crippling Covid-19 pandemic.

Navigating the post-independence years

In the post–Second World War global economy, the rupee was no
longer a currency of trade, as it had once been in the pre-colonial and
colonial Indian Ocean trade. In order to overcome slim forex reserves,
a largely inconvertible rupee, and bypass the US dollar's hegemony,
the innovation of rupee-denominated trade with the Soviet bloc
countries from 1948–1949 was introduced. But with one major difference: the bilateral trade was solely denominated in rupees.

Till 1958–1959, the difference between debits and credits in the rupee
accounts of these countries with the RBI had to be settled in a convertible
currency, like the sterling pound. After 1958–1959, this surplus was held
in these rupee accounts and any deficit was covered by overdrafts from
the RBI. The value of the Indian rupee in this trade was thereafter fixed in
terms of gold (Batliwalla 1998). The first set of these bilateral trade
agreements were executed with Yugoslavia, Czechoslovakia, Hungary
and Poland in 1948–1949. In the 1950s, agreements were signed with the
Soviet Union and other Eastern bloc countries. Trade with the region
increased rapidly, especially in the 1950s, from $9.2 million (1952–1953)
to $658 million (1965–1966), constituting just 0.3% at first and then
jumping to 14.2% of India's foreign trade.

The RBI managed the payments' structure mechanism of India's
trade with the Soviet bloc. As this trade was denominated in rupees,
each transacting country maintained three separate accounts with the
RBI, and one account with a commercial bank in India.

This rupee-denominated trade had major drawbacks, as numerous
RBI reports of this period indicate. It reduced earnings in hard currency;
a diversion of Indian goods from these countries to markets in the West;

and interest was being earned by these countries on current account balances in Indian commercial banks, whilst still drawing interest free rupee overdrafts from the RBI. The most glaring omission was highlighted when the rupee was devalued on 6 June 1966, due to a grave balance of payment crisis further aggravated in the aftermath of the 1965 India–Pakistan War. The gold clause was evoked by the Soviet Union, whereby the predetermined value of the rupee was fixed in terms of gold, a devaluation meant that the Soviet Union demanded additional payment in terms of rupees for their exports. As the price contracts did not allow for domestic price increases due to devaluation, Indian exporters were left exposed. This loophole in the Soviet bloc treaties was eventually settled through diplomatic channels.

Though the above is just one instance of the challenges India faced during the Cold War years, it was the 1991 forex crisis that forced the country to change tact from its Socialist inspired policies. Under the IMF's stringent conditions for its emergency loan to the country, much needed financial and capital market reforms were undertaken. The Indian rupee too was made partially convertible – only under current account but certain capital account transactions still need approval.

The positive fallout of these economic reforms has been that it has put the spotlight back on Bombay – today's Mumbai – because it is the financial capital of India. Where once politics drove the economy in the post-independence years, today largely economic imperatives drive politics like it once did in the colonial past. Not only is Mumbai the financial capital of India BUT the city hosts the country's major financial institutions – the RBI, BSE, National Stock Exchange, MCX (Multi-Commodity Exchange: Metals & Energy) and SEBI. It still retains its intrinsic strengths of skilled manpower, trading communities and historic microstructures like markets for everything produced in India and for much produced overseas, too. This is the reason why the plan in 2015 to make the city an IFC as recommended by the 2007 Percy Mistry Report, was greeted with great excitement. This has been shelved. Ahmedabad's Gujarat International Finance Tech-city (GIFT) will be India's first IFC or financial SEZ. But there is ample scope for another IFC – hopefully Mumbai will be its next location.

Notes

1 Calcutta maintained its lead over Bombay in subsequent years. Its decline began with the shifting of the British Indian capital to New Delhi in 1912. Post Indian independence, Bombay proved to be more resilient as a centre for trade, finance and industry.

2 The Gold Exchange Standard was established by 1899–1900 in order to control the exchange rate of the rupee vis-a-vis the sterling pound. During the war years, this standard broke down.
3 The only exception was made in the case of the Bank of Madras, for Ceylon – a British colony that was geographically contiguous to the Bank's area of business.

Bibliography

Bagchi, Amiya Kumar. 2007. *The Evolution of the State Bank of India: The Roots 1806–1876.* New Delhi: Penguin India.

Bagchi, Amiya Kumar. 1987. *The Evolution of the State Bank of India: The Roots 1806–1876.* New Delhi: Oxford University Press.

Batliwalla, C.J. 1998. "Bilateral Rupee Payment Agreements (Appendix G)." In *The Reserve Bank of India: 1951–1967,* by G. Balachandran., Ed. 846. New Delhi: Oxford University Press.

Bhandare, Shailendra. 2007. "Money on the Move: The Rupee and the Indian Ocean Region." In *Cross Currents and Community Networks: The History of the Indian Ocean World,* by Ray, Himanshu Prabha and Alpers, Edwards A. Eds. New Delhi: Oxford University Press.

Chandavarkar, A.G. 2013. "Money and Credit, 1857-1947." In *The Cambridge Economic History of India, Volume II: c. 1757–2003,* by Dharma Kumar, Tapan Raychaudhuri Ed., 762–803. New Delhi: Orient Blackswan in association with Cambridge University Press.

Dadabhoy, Bakhtiar K. 2013. *Barons of Banking: Glimpses of Indian Banking History.* Noida: Random House Publishers India Pvt. Ltd.

Edwardes, S.M., 1909. *The Gazetteer of Bombay City And Island.* 1977. Vol. 1. Bombay: Gazetteer Department Government of Maharashtra.

Ghadge, R. 2018.Connections and Disconnections: The making of Bombay/ Mumbai as India's "Global City."Journal of Global Initiatives: Policy, Pedagogy, Perspective 12(1), 5, https://digitalcommons.Kennesaw.edu/jgi/vol3/iso1/5

IMF. n.d. *Quota Reforms For a more representative, modern IMF (IMF Annual Report 2016).* Accessed June 23, 2021. https://www.imf.org/external/pubs/ft/ar/2016/eng/quota.htm.

Jackson, Stanley. 1968. *The Sassoons.* London: William Heinemann.

Jisc Archives Hub. n.d. "Oriental Bank Corporation." Accessed May 07, 2021. https://archiveshub.jisc.ac.uk/search/archives/bc488aca-8091-32b7–8e36-cf9b7299ee68.

Martin, Marina. 2009. "Hundi or Hawala: The Problem of Definition." *Modern Asian Studies* 43 (4): 909–937.

Nightingale, Pamela. Reprint 2008. *Trade And Empire In Western India 1784–1806.* New York: Cambridge University Press.

Overy, Richard. 2010. *The Times Complete History Of The World.* London: Harper Collins.

Shaikh, Bazil, interview by Lentin Sifra. 2013. *Bombay Rupee.*

Shaikh, Bazil. 2020. *The Conjuror's Trick: An Interpretive History of Paper Money in India.* Mumbai: The Marg Foundation.

Siddiqi, Asiya. 1982. "The Business World of Jamsetjee Jeejeebhoy." *Indian Economic & Social History Review* XIX (3 & 4): 301–324.

Suzuki, Toshio. 2012. "The Rise and Decline of the Oriental Bank Corporation, 1842-84." In *The Origins Of International Banking In Asia: The Nineteenth And Twentieth Centuries,* by Toshio Suzuki, Shizuya Nishimura, Ranald Michie Ed., 86–111. Great Britain: Oxford University Press.

6 Mercantile and a multicultural city

Bombay city attracted numerous foreign diplomatic missions in the 19th century, beginning with its oldest – and continuous – foreign mission, that of the United States, established in 1838. These diplomatic missions followed in the wake of increasing trade volumes between their nations and British India, then, and the setting up of related businesses by their merchants in the city, like banks, shipping lines, insurance and later, joint-venture manufacturing. The presence of this diplomatic corp. reached its apogee in the years 1870–1918, a time when the first global economy coalesced on the back of large parts of the world being European colonies. A declining Ottoman Empire during this period controlled the Middle East and North Africa, and had a consulate in Bombay till the outbreak of the First World War. It's role in the city's cultural life was unique as local Sunni Muslim communities looked to the Ottoman consulate general as a representative of their Caliph or *Sublime Porte,* as the Ottoman Sultan was referred to.

Though trade, trade-related matters and the issuance of visas were the main functions of these consulates then, just as they are today, what this chapter deals with is the profound influence that this consular presence and their expat population (excluding those dealt with in Chapter 4) had on the cultural life of the city. Trade with these nations will also be touched upon as it was the raison d'etre for these missions and their staff to be here in this city.

Parallel to this soft diplomacy and engagement between the consular corp. and the city's cognoscenti was a shift from a British sensibility in the arts and films to a European sensibility, especially French, German and Communist Soviet Union. The height of this period of experimentation was reached in the inter-war years, when European refugees escaping Nazism, settled temporarily in the city, infusing new ideas into Hindi film-making and mentoring the Bombay Progressive Artists Group.

DOI: 10.4324/9781003182894-6

Marxist Communism, whose epicentre in Europe during this period was Berlin had an impact on the local Indian Peoples Theatre Association, which was a training ground for many actors, dancers, musicians and directors, who became household names through Hindi films produced in the city.

This experimentation in films, theatre and the fine arts was a reflection of the rebalancing happening in the geopolitical sphere. The disintegration of the world's major empires after the First World War, and the creation of new nations, was what added not just to the political and economic churn but the intellectual one. From the imperial empires of Russia, the Ottoman, Prussia and the Austro-Hungarian, rose new nation like the Soviet Union, Austria, Hungary, Poland, the Baltic States, secular Turkey, Egypt, Iraq and Saudi Arabia.

Far more significant was the decline of the British Empire during this period and the accentuated nationalist movements within its colonies – like India.

It is in the context of global geopolitical realignments and their fallout, an accelerating Indian nationalist movement, and the impact both these parallel upheavals had on the cultural life of the city that the role of Bombay's consular corp. should be viewed.

Diplomats in the cultural palimpsest of Bombay

The first US Consulate General to be established on the Indian subcontinent was the one in Bombay on 12 October 1838. This anniversary is celebrated with great pomp every year by this Mission, as it was the first foothold that the Americans got, much before other European nations, in British India. The back story to the establishment of this first foreign diplomatic mission in Bombay was the 'Most Favoured Nation' (MFN) status bestowed on the United States in 1788, as an outcome of the American War of Independence (1775–1783) and the Treaty of Paris (1783) between Great Britain and its former 13 American colonies. This meant that the Americans were now 'free traders' who could sail into any British colonial port in spite of the existing EEIC monopoly over trade with both India and China. This had prevented private British traders from entering these markets till the Company's monopoly over the India and China trade ended in 1813 and 1833, respectively.

Trade preceded the establishment of this Consulate in the city, as it did in the case of most consulates, excepting that of the State of Israel, whose primary focus in its early years was to facilitate *Aliyah* (immigration) of the Indian Jews to the State of Israel. So, the nifty American clippers (ships of 400–600 tons), with their small crew and supercargo (business manager), were initially welcomed at British colonial ports, particularly Bombay and Surat, because they brought in huge amounts of silver specie (coins) in the early years in exchange for Surat piece goods (cloth). This silver was what the Company used to pay for its China trade and its mint at Bombay. For example, in 1804, American imports into these two ports were made up of Sicca rupee 207,564 of treasure, but only Sicca rupee 9,071 of merchandise (Milburn 1813).

The balance of trade began changing almost imperceptibly in favour of the Americans. Each voyage generated profits, with a clipper spending an average of one to three years, out on the Indian Ocean, laying anchor at port after port: 20% or more of the proceeds had to go to its investors. American merchants not only stumbled upon the profitability of the intra-Asian trade, like the Dutch East India Company (VOC) before it, BUT the profitability of trading in Deccan short staple cotton, indigo, ginger and saltpetre (potassium nitrate used in gunpowder), and later Malwa opium, all sourced from Bombay. Furthermore, they expanded this sphere of trade beyond the Indian Ocean by selling goods at various ports in Europe, the Caribbean and South America, as the American market was too small to absorb the volume of this trade.

These networks of trade were engendered by necessity, like the time Elias Haskett Derby – America's first millionaire who made his fortune trading in Deccan cotton sourced from Bombay – had to divert his first shipment of Deccan cotton ever to the United States – carried aboard his clipper 'Grand Turk' in 1787–1788 – to Canton (Guangzhou), where there was a ready market for it. Now, having stumbled on this valuable country trade in Deccan cotton from Bombay to Canton, he backed this up by purchasing more raw cotton at Bombay and sending it directly to Canton, where he exchanged it for Chinese tea and silks. Simultaneously, the Americans' import of silver specie into Bombay almost stopped by the first decade of the 19th century as goods that they brought in, such as brandy, claret and port wine; metals; cordage, oil and sugar, generated for them the money to buy cotton, and later opium, in Bombay, for the China market.

Almost parallel to the appointment in 1838 of the first US Consul Philemon S. Parker – who was **not** given official recognition by the Company's government in Bombay[1] – was the beginning of the large-scale import of American ice into the city. Initially, this ice was consumed by the cognoscenti, as illustrated by the stir that the first consignment to Bombay in 1834 created.

The arrival of this consignment, given the nature of the commodity, was allowed to bypass customs. It was unloaded at night to prevent melting, and its consumption (as reported by the Gujarati newspaper *Bombay Samachar*) at a party hosted by Jamsetjee Jeejeebhoy, merchant and philanthropist, resulted in the host and his guests coming down with a cold the next day (Dwivedi and Mehrotra 1995). The recipient of the first consignment of ice was Jehangir Nusserwanjee Wadia, the son of Nusserwanjee Maneckjee Wadia, a merchant who transacted all American business in the city, then.

This did not dampen the enthusiasm for American ice in the city, with an ice committee being setup to supervise its storage and distribution, and an ice house being built in 1843 outside the Naval Dockyard gate at the same spot where the K.R. Cama Oriental Institute now stands.

The lucrative American ice trade began first with its export to Calcutta in 1833, and the following year to Bombay. It was advantageous to American merchants once Boston businessman Frederick Tudor devised a way to transport large blocks of ice across the Atlantic Ocean into Indian Ocean ports – a voyage of four months – by devising a way of insulating the holds of clippers and wrapping the thick blocks of ice harvested from the frozen ponds of Boston and its vicinity, with pine dust and wrapping them in felt. The ice provided much-needed ballast to the clippers on their long journey to India, moreover it could be sold profitably generating capital to buy goods in Bombay, for their onwards journey to China. The ice trade ended in the 1880s, with ice factories being set up in Bombay. In one sense, it marked the transition of American trade – from its early years, when it enjoyed MFN status – to when tariff barriers were set up by both sides to protect a nascent American and Bombay cotton mill industry.

Two enduring symbols to the almost 200-year presence of the American Consulate General in Bombay was its former office-cum-residence at Lincoln House (former Wankaner House) on the Breach Candy sea front, from 1957 to 2015, and the American Center Library (renamed Dosti House), which was inaugurated on 23 November 1944, on Thanksgiving Day. The library is now part of the US Information Service (USIS), but was formerly part of the Office of War Information, originally located in the former National City Bank of New York (now Citibank) premises on Hornby Road (Dadabhai Naoroji Road). Today, both the library and the offices of this Consulate General have shifted to common premises at the Bandra Kurla Complex.

In contrast to the United States, the Consulate General of Turkey – originally established as the Imperial Ottoman Consulate in 1849 – was deeply engaged in the religious and cultural life of Bombay's Sunni Muslim communities. The vast Ottoman Empire (1258–1908) straddled present-day Egypt, Syria, Israel, Palestine, Lebanon, Jordan, Iraq, Saudi Arabia and the Persian Gulf region, largely populated by Arab tribes. Trade between Bombay and the Ottoman Empire was carried on through the age-old *dhow* trade. It was a trade dominated by Arabian horses, Basra pearls, food grains, coffee, sugar candy, cotton piece goods, dried fruits and dates.

The Ottoman Caliph was then the spiritual and temporal head of the global Sunni Islamic world, hence his diplomatic representative in Bombay was an important personage among local Sunni Muslims and trading communities from Ottoman territories, like the Arab and Baghdadi merchants resident in this city. Given these strong trade linkages, it wasn't surprising that traders around the Hejaz made a representation to the Ottoman Sultan Abdulmecid (who reigned from 1839–1861), through the governor of Jiddah, to establish a consulate in Bombay.

Documents from the Ottoman archives indicate that Hadji Jeyb was the first Ottoman consul in Bombay in 1849. Another early consul was the Basra trader Timurzade Abdulvahap Aga, who was resident in Bombay. His appointment points to the Basra-Baghdad trade with Bombay being a vital part of the Consulate's work.

Whilst trade was important, a source of contention between the Bombay Ottoman consulate with British authorities in both Bombay and Jiddah was its issuance of visas to Muslim pilgrims from different corners of Asia (Bukhara, Turkestan-Kashgar) and the subcontinent, who congregated in Bombay to embark on ships and *dhows* headed to Jiddah. The outbreak of the cholera and plague epidemics during the annual Haj, and its transmission to Europe, was often blamed on those embarking from Bombay. Another contentious issue was the radicalisation of these pilgrims during the month-long Haj.

It is not entirely clear where the office of the Imperial Ottoman consulate was located in the city. The correspondence of one of the most famous Ottoman consuls in Bombay, Abdül Haq Hâmid (1883–1885), indicates that the consulate was located in the Fort precinct. A professional diplomat, Hâmid, remains a celebrated Turkish poet, and is regarded as the founder of modern Turkish dramatic poetry (Ergen 2015).

The outbreak of World War I resulted in the house arrest of the last Ottoman consul Basri Bey, and later his deportation to a POW camp. It was only after the war in 1918 that he was swapped for the British ex-consul of Basra. After the war, Turkish interests in the city were looked after by the Swedish Consulate and then the Netherlands' Consulate. There was a long hiatus, even after the establishment of the

Republic of Turkey in 1923, before the consulate was reopened in Bombay. An honorary Republic of Turkey consulate was opened in 1940; however, the first honorary consul, Rahim Karim Mistry, was appointed only in 1953. It is not clear from available sources when the first career diplomat was appointed, and when the consulate was upgraded to a consulate general.

While the Imperial Ottoman Consulate had a unique role among local Muslim communities in Bombay, especially in the religious sphere as the Islamic world's holiest sites were located in this Empire and the Caliph was its designated caretaker, the old European consulates introduced a cultural perspective that differed from the British colonial one, bringing in refreshing new ideas in the arts, literature, theatre, films, sciences and even ideologies.

Bombay's oldest European consulates

The oldest European consulates in Bombay is that of the Prussian Honorary Consulate (est. 1856) – the predecessor of the Consulate General of the Federal Republic of Germany in Mumbai – and that of the Hanseatic State of Hamburg,[2] established in 1844. The Kingdom of Prussia was the largest state in a loose confederation of German-speaking states (including Austria) from 1815 to 1866.

The impetus to establish these missions was largely to oversee and promote trade between the states of Prussia and Hamburg with Bombay. The first honorary consul of Prussia was F. Matthey, who was appointed in 1856, and was probably a merchant in the city. In 1862, the third consul for Hamburg, August Carl Gumpert (1859–1868), also assumed charge of the Prussian consulate.

By all accounts, the capital city of British India – Calcutta – remained the focus of the German diplomatic mission both in terms of business (the Bengal–Burma–Thai rice trade) and cultural relations. In these early years, the focus of the honorary consul in Bombay was more as a representative of and facilitator for German business interests. One indication of this is a report by the German Consul (Bombay) of 1870, which records 11 German ships anchored in Bombay, whose home ports were Bremen, Hamburg, Danzig and the English port of Hull. These ships, like the American clippers, were also engaged in the intra-Asian trade, having arrived from ports as varied as Bushire, Rangoon, Bangkok, New Castle (in Australia), Glasgow, Liverpool, Newcastle (in England), Cardiff and Hamburg. Commodities carried on board included roasted coffee, wheat, cotton and rice. A major commodity taken on board at Bombay was raw cotton. This sizeable presence of German shipping was indicative that Bombay was an important destination and transshipment port for them.

It was only as late as 1886[3] that the *Reichstag* (the Lower House) under German Chancellor Otto von Bismarck decided to post a professional diplomat to Bombay. This made Consul Heinrich Bartels (1887–1888) the first career German consul in Bombay. By then the relationship between Germany and Bombay became more nuanced. German manufacturing had already reached India through Siemens, which constructed the first telegraph line connecting Calcutta to London between 1868 and 1870. Siemens also built one of Bombay's earliest power plants in 1912, for Tata Power's Khopoli hydroelectric plant.[4] And the city already had a resident German merchant and missionary population. German missionaries were most notably associated as teachers in St. Xavier's College and School, both located at Dhobi Talao in South Bombay.

In 1901, the German consulate's office was located on the corner of Henry Road (in Colaba) and Apollo Bunder Road. Its jurisdiction then included Bombay Presidency, the district of Mangalore (part of Madras Presidency), Central Provinces, the Princely States in both these regions, and the Nizam of Hyderabad's dominions. It also had supervisory control over the German consular authorities in Aden and Karachi.

Geopolitical upheavals with the outbreak of the First World War (1914–1918) and the Second World War (1939–1945) made Germany an enemy country in British India. It led to the closure of the Bombay Consulate, the internment of German nationals and the sealing of German properties as 'enemy' ones. Though the end of both wars led to a quick resumption of diplomatic ties in 1921, in the aftermath of the first war in particular, industry and trade associations – like the Bombay Chamber of Commerce – re-admitted German companies only as late as 1929.

It is in these inter-war years, as discussed later in this chapter, that had the most profound cultural influence through the return of Indians who had studied and worked in Germany, and the resident German expatriate and refugee population.

What is noteworthy is the early impact of imported German manufactured goods in India, particularly that of German cars. In a *Report of the German Consulate in Bombay Concerning the Economic Situation in Western India* (12 December 1935), a broad overview of trade between Western India and Germany from 1914 to 1934–1935 is given. The import of machinery from Germany for the cotton mill industry and the sugar cane industry are especially notable.[5] An import that made its appearance around this time was German cars. Initially, of the 7,266 cars imported in 1935, only 134 were from Germany but this kept increasing. The Maharaja of Kolhapur's luxury limousine, the Maybach SW42, 1935, is possibly the oldest German car in India, a luxury brand that has resurfaced as the Mercedes-Benz S-Class under the Maybach label.

Just before the closure of this Consulate on the eve of the Second World War, it was upgraded to a Consulate General in 1938, and was given an extended jurisdiction that included Sind; Rajputana; and Portuguese-ruled Goa, Daman and Diu. After Independence in 1947, India was the first country in the world to re-establish diplomatic relations with the Federal Republic of Germany (West Germany). The first consul general to be assigned to Bombay was a German Jew, Franz Mendelssohn von Theodor Heuss, in 1951.

It was only after 1951 that the institutionalised cultural ecosystem between Bombay and Germany took root, like the Max Mueller Bhavan and the Goethe Institute in Fort, and the German School Mumbai and DAAD, for academic exchange services. What truly celebrates the Bombay–Germany relationship is the 1968 city-twinning between Bombay and Stuttgart, the home city for Mercedes-Benz and the ritzy Lamborghini sports cars, both favourites among Mumbai's rich. Bombay city then, with its textile mills, petrochemical and electronics industries, was a major Indian manufacturing hub. More fittingly perhaps is Stuttgart's annual Festival of Indian Films, to celebrate the sheer diversity of films made in India, most of them in Mumbai's prolific films industry, where German influence was strongly felt during the inter-war years.

Another country that exerted a strong cultural influence, particularly over the city's anglicised Parsi community, was France.

Like most foreign missions, trade preceded the setting up of a Consulat Général de France á Bombay in 1865. In spite of the intermittent Anglo-French conflicts in Europe, which often spilt over to the Indian subcontinent, French shipping increasingly began using Bombay port instead of Surat, en route their colonies on the Indian Subcontinent's east coast – Pondicherry,[6] Yanam, Karaikal, Chandernagore – and onwards to French Indo-China (today's Laos, Cambodia, Vietnam), which was the focus of their trade during the 19th century (Perrin 2015).

One indication of this is the migration of Sir Dinshaw Petit's grandfather, Nasarvanji Kavasji, to Bombay in 1785. As a shipping agent and *dubash* (interpreter) for all French shipping that passed through Bombay, he was referred to by French ship officers as *le petit*

Parsi (the petite Parsi), which was soon shortened to the nickname Petit (Edwardes 1923). It is this nickname that his son Manockjee and grandson Sir Dinshaw, both pioneers of Bombay's cotton mill industry, adopted as their surname.

By the mid-19th century, France's business engagement with the city was important enough for it to open a consulate in 1865, barely four years before the Suez Canal that the French built. The dramatic shortening of the sea route to the east from Europe in 1869 catapulted Bombay into an important financial and diplomatic hub. France's first consul to Bombay was Monsieur Albert Thenon, whose letter of appointment was signed by Napoleon III.

It is clear that very few French people were resident in the city in 1865, though the French bank, *Comptoir National D'Escompte* (today's BNP Paribas) had a branch as early as 1861, and the Lyon-headquartered shipping company, *Messageries Maritime*, also had a presence in the city.

What was incredible about this small presence was the interest the city's cognoscenti took in learning the French language, literature and putting up performances of plays by French playwrights, like Molière. A remnant of this past is the still functioning, and probably, oldest, private French library in India – *Le Cercle Littéraire* – located in the Kala Ghoda precinct of Fort. It was established in 1886 by one Mr Davar, originally as *Le Cercle Franco-Parsi de Bombay* or the Franco-Parsi Literary Circle, a fitting name given that Parsi youth in particular were attracted to French culture (Mehta and Davar 2017). By the late 19th century, there were a few British, Jews, Portuguese Christians, Muslims and Hindus too.

Another venerable institution in the city with its vast network of French classes is the 109-year-old *Alliance Français,* established in the city in 1912 by the French government to teach French and promote French culture. Although run federally, like the German cultural institutions, the *Alliance Français* along with the highlight of Bastille Day (or National Day) celebrations hosted annually by the Consulate on 14 July, almost since its establishment, form a rich French cultural ecosystem in the city.

What sustains this cultural overlay, however, is the thriving centuries-old business relationship between Mumbai and France. Where once spices and cotton attracted French shipping to the city, it is defence deals, like the manufacturing of the French Scorpene submarines at Mumbai's Mazagaon Docks Ltd. which makes this relationship strategic.[7]

Honorary consuls: facilitating trade

An often-seen figure in Bombay's business world from the mid-19th century to about the first half of the 20th century, were the European merchants, representatives of the foreign trading houses. One merchant in particular, who was a key facilitator and honorary consul to three countries – Sweden and Norway, and the Netherlands – before a Bombay representative of his firm was appointed as honorary consul for his home country Switzerland – was Johannes Georg Volkart, the India partner of the Swiss trading house of Volkart Brothers, which is today the Mumbai headquartered Voltas India Ltd.[8]

The chronology in which Volkart was appointed as honorary consul of these three countries, has a history of its own. Much is not known about these missions in the early years, but it is significant that Sweden and Norway have reopened their consulates in 2012 and 2015, respectively, and this time with full-time career diplomats heading them, which was not the case earlier.

Another notable feature is that their trade with the Indian subcontinent led to the establishment early on of some of the most respected multinational companies in India today. Most of these companies, true to their transnational character, are today largely headed by Indians in India where once they had Europeans only in top management in the pre-independence years.

The establishment of the Consulate General of the Kingdom of The Netherlands in Bombay in 1856 followed the setting up of a diplomatic mission by the Netherlands earlier in Calcutta, the British Indian capital city. This followed an agreement between the Netherlands and Great Britain, allowing for consular representation across the British Empire in Africa, Asia, America and Australia.

Notably, the Dutch East India Company (VOC) in the 17th and 18th centuries was a fierce competitor to the English Company. By the time of this Agreement in the 19th century, the VOC had been wound up following its bankruptcy in 1795, and its colonies and trading outposts in India and South East Asia were handed over to the Dutch government, and were collectively known as the Dutch East Indies. Compared to Great Britain, the Netherlands was a much diminished power after the Napoleonic Wars (1795–1813), during which time its country was run over by France. Although its colonies in the east were given back to the Netherlands by Great Britain[9] under the Treaty of Paris (1783), it wasn't long when all the VOC's colonies, like Cochin, Chinsurah, Ceylon (Sri Lanka) and Dutch Batavia (old Jakarta) were handed to the British under the 'Treaty of London' (1824).

The first honorary consul of the Netherlands was Johannes Georg Volkart, a Swiss merchant based in Bombay and the co-founder of the Winterthur-based Swiss trading firm of Volkart Brothers. The appointment of Volkart as the Dutch honorary consul, and soon after as the honorary consul for Sweden and Norway (they separated in 1905) in Bombay on 7 September 1858, brings into sharp focus that facilitating trade and economic diplomacy was the criteria for all three countries.

Much before a Swiss Consulate was established in the city in 1915, the first five honorary consuls of the Netherlands were all Swiss and from the trading firm of Volkart Brothers. It was only from the sixth consul Carl Wilhelm Freese, a German and a director of Holland Bombay Trading Co. Ltd, that a Dutch firm took over the reins at this Consulate.[10]

Volkart Brothers (Bombay) was founded on 1 February 1851, on the same day as its parent firm Gebrüder Volkart was founded in Winterthur (Switzerland). It appears Volkart Brothers was also the first Swiss firm to see the huge potential in carrying out a sea-borne trade with the East. Switzerland is a land-locked country, but since the early 13th century was strategically located on an important north-south trade route that cut through the Alps and connected the then remote regions of northern Europe with the sea-faring Mediterranean countries. From this period onwards, Switzerland reaped the benefits of overseas trade and the Industrial Revolution, becoming in 1850 the second-most industrialised country after Britain (Switzerland History n.d.).

What led eventually to the establishment of an honorary Swiss Consulate in Bombay on 15 May 1915 was the outbreak of the First World War in 1914. The Swiss Confederation (Switzerland) did not feel the need to appoint a consul earlier, as official intervention with the British Indian government was usually conducted through the German consulate in Bombay. With the outbreak of War, the German consulate was closed. As Bombay was an important source of raw cotton for the Swiss textile industry, it made sense to open a diplomatic mission here. Consequently, the King's Exequatur was issued by the foreign office to the Swiss Legation in London, appointing Karl Ringger (resident manager of Volkart Brothers, Bombay) as the first Swiss Honorary Consul. The choice of Honorary Consul Ringger was made in light of the fact that Volkart Brothers was the biggest, most powerful and the first Swiss firm to establish trade between Bombay and Switzerland. By this time too, there were other prominent Swiss firms headquartered in Bombay like Geilinger & Blum, Wattenbach & Heligers and Nestle (Bienz 2015).

As Switzerland maintained its neutrality during both world wars – just as it does even today [11] – its Consulate in Bombay looked after German interests in the city during the war years. Just before the outbreak of the First World War, there were 40 Swiss nationals' resident in Bombay city, which included missionaries from both the Catholic and the Protestant church – Switzerland being home to both churches.

It appears that the Swedish, Norwegian, Dutch and Swiss consulates, all functioned with honorary consuls chosen from among the heads of their companies headquartered in Bombay. The Swiss Consul Ringger took the title of Consul General, when the Swiss mission in the city was upgraded to a Consulate General in 1921, due to his increased responsibilities during the War. It is unclear, when the Swiss consulate general in Bombay acquired a career diplomat to head it, but the first career diplomat to head the city's Dutch consulate general was Eyland Frederick Maurits van Hall in 1956.

Diplomacy, films and art in the inter-war years

The inter-war years from 1918 to 1939 were a period of frenetic activity and political and intellectual upheaval in Bombay. Mahatma Gandhi on his return from South Africa in 1915 made the city his headquarters from 1917 to 1934, launching his first Non-cooperation Movement and the Khilafat Movement from here. His biggest supporters being Gujarati traders from the city's wholesale markets. Almost parallel to this was the establishment of the Communist Party of India (CPI) headquartered in the city – founded during the Second COMINTERN (Communist International Conference) held in Tashkent in 1925. However, it was the CPI's cultural wing – the Indian Peoples Theatre Association or IPTA (established 1942) – also founded in the city, which had a direct influence on the city's cultural ecosystem.

The IPTA's impromptu street plays based on proletarian themes were a common sight outside the gates of textile mills during the longest ever pre-independence labour unrest of the 1940s, as were its troupes of street singers who went round the city collecting money, grain and clothes for the victims of the Bengal Famine of 1942.

The importance of the IPTA lies in the alternative narrative and sensibility it engendered, when compared to the popular Company (British) theatre, Parsi theatre and the many travelling European troupes that visited the Subcontinent. It's plays drew inspiration from European Expressionist theatre and art in set design, Russian Agitprop theatre, and its choice of playwrights were largely from the

Soviet Bloc countries. Significantly, along with writers from the Progressive Writers Association (PWA), founded by a group of left-wing writers eight years earlier, the IPTA formed a creative and ex-perimental hub where some of the city's Hindi film industry's most successful actors, writers and directors first earned their spurs.

It was in this political, social and cultural churn of the inter-war years and the Second World War that innumerable German and German-speaking refugees made Bombay their home, resulting in an intellectual and cultural renaissance in the city. Their contribution to Bombay's film industry and the Progressive Artists Group (PAG) has been stellar in terms of mentoring, showcasing local talent and even direct contribution to these fields.

But it is to another city beginning with 'B' – Berlin – then the cul-tural capital of Europe, and also where Adolf Hitler's brown-necks clashed violently with the Communists on its streets, that one must look to in order to understand almost everything that transpired in Bombay during these years.

Berlin and Bombay: the two Bs

In the aftermath of the First World War, when a defeated Germany was rebuilding itself under the Weimar Republic (1919–1933), its ca-pital city of Berlin became the scientific and cultural hub of Continental Europe. There was an edgy creativity palpable in Berlin because of the charged political atmosphere then prevalent. It was both the nerve centre for Communism in Europe, and its opposite number – a resurgent German right-wing, militaristic nationalism – which often led to violent clashes on its streets.

It was during this time – the 1920s and 1930s – that numerous Indian artists visited and worked in Berlin. Some well-known names from Bombay were directors Mohan Bhavnani and Himanshu Rai, and actress Devika Rani, who all trained and worked in Berlin's Universum-Film-Aktiengesellschaft (Ufa), a grouping of Germany's leading film studios. In Vienna, during the same period, a young Parsi art student, Silloo Vimadalal, who was studying painting under Professor Walter Langhammer, became responsible for bringing him and his wife to Bombay.

Such friendships and connections made Bombay a refuge for a number of Jews fleeing Fascism in Europe. It was then imperative for each immigrant to have a guarantor to vouch for his or her political affiliations and permanent maintenance in British India. Although this was substantively amended in late 1938 by the India Office (London), numerous conditions had to be fulfilled before immigrants, and later, refugees, were allowed into British India.

Just before the Second World War began, there were 2153 registered foreigners resident in Bombay. This number excluded consular staff and children (below 16 years). Of this total, 1051 were European (550 of them Germans), 886 Asiatics (from Afghanistan, Bukhara, Central Asia), 211 Americans, and 5 Africans (Bhatti and Johannes 2005).

European cultural influences in Bombay

The European influence, as distinct from the British one, was of two types: those who brought back new ideas from Europe, like Mohan Bhavnani, Himanshu Rai and his wife Devika Rani, and implemented them in Bombay with the help of their immigrant friends; and European immigrants who had a profound influence on local art, music and film-making.

In the first category, when Himanshu Rai and Devika Rani returned to Bombay from Germany in 1934, with the Hindi version of their talkie film, *Karma*, directed by Franz Osten, and produced as an Indo-British collaboration,[12] they also set up in the same year the city's first professionally run film studio, Bombay Talkies, in Malad, a suburb of north Bombay, modelled on Berlin's Ufa studios. It was at Bombay Talkies that Rai's director, Franz Osten, and cameraman, Helmut Wirching, both worked before they were interned at a camp in Ahmednagar during the war years.

Bombay Talkies was the first professionally run film studio in the city to introduce a structured internship programme unlike the informal apprenticeships prevalent then. It was here that many luminaries of the film industry were trained, including actors Ashok Kumar, Raj Kapoor, Dilip Kumar, Sashadhar Mukerjee (film producer and one of three founders of Filmistan Studios) and Khwaja Ahmed Abbas (well-known script-writer and director of Raj Kapoor's films). The latter also belonged to the PWA-IPTA, and was closely associated with actor-director Raj Kapoor, whose films, like *Awaara* and *Mera Naam Joker,* he scripted.

Director Mohan Bhavnani, whose early films include *Mazdoor* (English title: The Mill, 1934) and *Jagran* (The Awakening, 1935), both considered too provocative because of labour unrest across India in the 1930s and early 1940s was the guarantor for music composer Walter Kaufmann and scriptwriter Willy Haas (Gangar 2013).

Kaufmann is well known for composing the signature tune for All India Radio, but his most significant contribution was the introduction of orchestral music, using Indian musical instruments, into Hindi films and documentaries made by Information Films of India, a precursor to Films Division of India.

Another significant contribution was that of a core group of immigrants – Walter Langhammer (mentor and teacher) and his wife Kathë (who became secretary of the Bombay Art Society), Rudy Von Leyden (art critic and cartoonist at *TheTimes of India*) and Emmanuel Schlesinger (art collector). These Europeans mentored the artistic growth of Bombay's Progressive Artists Group (PAG), whose original members were F.N. Souza, M.F. Husain, S.H. Raza, S.H. Gade, K.H. Ara and S.K. Bakre.

The impetus to move away from the realism of the British academic school of art and revivalism of the Ajanta fresco style was already under way in the city when the PAG began coalescing in the early 1940s. What the Europeans did was to expose the group to different modern – predominantly Western – schools of art, like Expressionism, at the weekly Sunday salons held at the Langhammer home on Nepean Sea Road, and provide the members informed feedback on their work.

Though most of Bombay's German-speaking immigrants left the city by the 1960s and early 1970s, their cultural legacy was the internationalism that was so much a part of the city then. Whilst these Europeans found refuge in the city during the war years and after, many others like the Polish refugees had to be searched and rescued by overland missions sent to the Soviet Union by their consulate in Bombay.

The Polish Consulate's search and rescue missions

The history of Bombay's Polish consulate is unique on many counts. Established in 1933, it was the first Polish consulate to be established in Asia, after the formation of Poland in 1918, after the First World War.

Second, though the consulate in Bombay was established for the purpose of building trade between Poland and the East, the intervention of the Second World War and the invasion of Poland from the West by Germany (on 1 September 1939) and from the East by the USSR (on 17 September 1939) *transformed* the role of the consulate in Bombay.

In its early years (1933–1939), the Polish consulate was preoccupied with trade. This was largely in agricultural products, pharmaceuticals and machinery and tools imported from Poland. Exports from India were mostly rice and spices (Leszek 2015). The consulate's status was stepped up to consulate general in early 1939, just months before the outbreak of the Second World War. Even after the invasion of Poland, the consulate never closed its offices in the city, which were then located at Nepean Sea Road.

During the war, the consulate continued to represent the Polish government-in-exile in London, headed by General Wladyslaw Sikorski. The main focus of the Bombay consulate's work during these war years was to 'search and rescue' the thousands of Polish children, women and elderly who were released from the Soviet *gulags* (prison camps), when the USSR joined the Allies in 1940. Some estimates state that the Soviets deported between 1.6 and 2.2 million Poles as slave labour to the prison camps and recruited young men forcibly into the Red Army (Glazer, et al. 2002).

With the USSR joining the Allied war efforts, Polish prisoners were slowly released. The young men joined hastily formed Polish regiments, while women, children and the elderly became refugees. It was from Bombay that the Polish Consulate General Dr Eugeniusz Banasiński, the consulate staff (notably the press attaché Wanda Dynowska, named Umadevi by Mahatma Gandhi), and the consul general's wife, Kira (a representative of the Polish Red Cross), set about organising two overland expeditions from Bombay into the Soviet Central Asian states of Kazakhstan and Turkmenistan.

The First Expedition from Bombay, which consisted of a convoy of trucks carrying essential supplies, reached the Soviet Union in late 1941 and carried back the first batch of Polish children to Bombay in mid-1942. The children were temporarily housed in the city before they were sent to the Balachadi Camp hosted by the princely State of Nawanagar on the Kutch Peninsula. Another major refugee camp was in Valivade in the then princely state of Kolhapur.

Arranging the finance, overseeing the administration and logistics of not just the camps but older children studying at the St. Mary's Boys Institution in Bombay, and for the Polish girls studying in a Convent School in Panchgani, was the Consulate in Bombay.

However, after the November 1943 Tehran Conference, the British government withdrew support for the Polish government-in-exile. This transition was managed by the consulate general in Bombay by converting itself into a mission of the Polish Red Cross, in order to continue looking after the refugees under its care till they were resettled in their final destination.

According to a report of 1945, there were 5577 Polish refugees in India being looked after through the agency of the consulate general in

Bombay (Glazer, et al. 2002). The city also hosted the Polish Red Cross Hospital on Queens Road, which was inaugurated in June 1944. The hospital was set up for people from the Polish camps, but was open to all patients subject to availability of beds.

Other notable organisations associated with this consulate were the Federation of Poles in India (formed by the early refugees of 1940–1941), and the Indo-Polish Library in the consulate's premises – which survived till 1976 (Glazer, et al. 2002).

This consulate general, however, closed down in September 1945, and did not reopen till 1963 at Manavi Apartment on Malabar Hill. One shipping line that kept the Polish presence alive in the city till the early 21st century was Polish Shipping Lines, whose office was located at Horniman Circle.

After the war and Indian independence

With the end of the Second World War in 1945, followed by Indian independence on 15 August 1947, there was a global restructuring which broadly arranged the world into two power blocs, one led by the United States and the other by the Soviet Union. This and India's post-independent socialist model of development that was formally adopted under the Second Five-Year Plan (1956–1961) had a dampening effect on trade and business with Bombay.

Most consulates that had been established in the late 19th century closed down in the 1960s, but have reopened in the city since the 2010s. These were largely countries, like Czechoslovakia, Finland, Norway, Spain and Italy, who had trade rather than manufacturing joint ventures with Indian promoters. Some have reopened with honorary consuls representing them, but recently Norway, Spain and Italy have reopened their consulates, with career diplomats heading them.

China closed down its consulate with the outbreak of the India–China war of 1962, reopening its consulate in the city only 30 years later. Japan, whose consulate in Bombay (established on 25 November 1894) was its first diplomatic mission in British India, closed briefly during the Second World War but reopened shortly thereafter once again in Bombay as a Japanese liaison office in 1950. The Consulate General of Japan in Bombay was reopened in 1952.

This reopening marked a new phase in Bombay–Japan relations, as it also marked the entry of Japanese companies into India, initially in the Bombay Poona region. Though Japanese focus later shifted to iron-ore mining in Goa in the 1950s and 1960s, then the Delhi–Haryana belt with the setting up of Maruti Suzuki in the 1980s, and now Bengaluru for its start-ups, Bombay is once again its focus with the Japan International Cooperation Agency (JICA)-aided Mumbai Metro Rail Corporation, which is going to transform the way city dwellers travel. The Japanese cultural impact though will always be part of the city's DNA, given the history of Japan's early expat population in the city (see chapter 4).

New consulates, like that of the State of Israel, was set up in 1950, at first with an honorary consul, till the first career consul was appointed in 1953. The main focus of this consulate, till political relations between India and Israel was normalised in 1992, was the mélange of Indian Jewish communities and the many refugee Jews – Iraqis, Afghan and European Jews – who sought safety in Bombay during the inter-war years. The main function of this consulate then was facilitating *Aliyah* (the right of every Jew to return to the Holy Land) for these Jews if they wished to settle in Israel (Akov 2015). Since the normalisation of relations with Israel, the responsibilities of this diplomatic mission today span all the things that consulates do – trade, defence, technology, education, tourism and cultural diplomacy.

While Mumbai today has recouped its diplomatic corp. and importance, with the liberalisation and reforms of the Indian economy since 1991, its role is set to change given new trends.

First, as the financial capital of India, home to the largest number of Indian billionaires, and the headquarters of the country's largest companies (Reliance and the Tata group of companies), most consulates are looking to attract investments from Mumbai to their countries, making their diplomatic mission in Mumbai a tactical one.

Second, though city-to-city diplomacy or city twinning is a relatively old concept with roots in the 1950s (Bombay's first city twinning was with Los Angeles), this para-diplomacy has gained traction since the late 20th century with China leveraging it very astutely in every sphere – infrastructure, business, education and people-to-people relations (culture). Even otherwise the role of cities in para-diplomacy is growing exponentially as underscored by the 2015 COP21 climate talks in Paris, when 30 American city mayors attended the Paris talks in their capacity as mayors of their city.

Lastly, Mumbai's greatest strength is its multicultural social fabric. The latter has been the grist for its flourishing film industry and its internationally recognised art, music and literary legacies. Mumbai's multicultralism makes it not just an important mercantile city BUT a truly international one!

Notes

1 The first American career diplomat to gain British recognition was Edward Ely, who received his appointment orders on 9 January 1851. The US Consulate General in Mumbai celebrate 1838 as their founding year instead of 1851.
2 The concept of the European Union traces its beginnings to the many Hanseatic States (most prominent were Hamburg, Luebek, Hanover, Bremen) that existed in Northern Europe since the Medieval Ages. These states were sovereign states, who had voluntarily bound themselves into a loose federation based on the common interests of trade and commerce.
3 The Prussian Honorary Consulate in Bombay was renamed the Consulate of the North German Confederation in 1868, after the earlier German Confederation (that included Austria) was dissolved in the aftermath of the Austro-Prussian War of 1866. The consulate once again changed its name to the Imperial German Consulate after the founding of the German Empire (*Deutsches Reich*) in 1871. The appointment of the first career consul happened in the latter period.
4 Other early entrants to the city were German companies Hoechst, Bayer, BASF, I.G. Farben and Bosch. Bayer India Ltd. and BASF are both headquartered in the city today.
5 This information was shared with the author by the Consulate General of the Federal Republic of Germany in Mumbai.
    Some of the major goods imported from Germany (1934–1935) as a percentage of total Indian imports.

Machinery	11%	Dyestuffs	73%
Metals (excluding mineral ores)	17%	Paper	12%
Ironmongery (excluding Cutlery)	32%	Chemicals, drugs & medicines	18%
Electrical instruments	11%		

Source: 'Report of the German Consulate in Bombay concerning the economic situation in Western India' (12 December 1935).

6 Pondicherry remained a French enclave till 1954, much after Indian independence in 1947.
7 Bilateral defence deals form the bulk of Indo-French trade. According to the author's interview of 2015 with the then Consul General and the French press attaché, 400 French companies have investments in India, through 1,000 branches that employ 300,000 employees. The largest of these is the info-tech giant based in Pune, Capgemini. Over 40% of French companies are invested in the State of Maharashtra.
8 Volkart Bros. and Tatas merged in 1952 to form Voltas India Ltd.
9 Britain had administered the Dutch colonies during the Napoleonic Wars.
10 The first Dutchman to be appointed consul was Jacques Bendien, at first an agent of the Holland Bombay Trading Co., and later the founder of Grimm & Bendien, which traded in textiles, chemicals, metal and glass from the city.

11 Trade and investments between India and Switzerland are conducted on a bilateral basis, as Swiss federalism and neutrality do not permit it to be part of the EU, NATO or any economic, political or military grouping with the exception of the Schengen. Switzerland became a member of the World Bank and IMF only in 1992 and of the UN in 2002.

12 Himanshu Rai co-produced and directed his first three films (*The Light of Asia*, 1925;*Shiraz*,1928; and *A Throw of Dice*, 1929) with Emelka Studios, Germany. In fact, *Light of Asia* was the first Indo-German film collaboration. The deteriorating political situation in Germany made it difficult for him to raise finance in Germany for his film *Karma* (1933).

Bibliography

1935. "Report of the German Consulate in Bombay concerning the economic situation in Western India."

Akov, Consul General of Israel David, interview by Sifra Lentin. 2015. *History of Bombay–Israel Relations* (October 23).

Bhatti, Anil, Johannes H. Voigt Eds. 2005. *Jewish Exile In India 1933–1945*. New Delhi: Manohar and Max Mueller Bhavan New Delhi.

Bienz, Swiss Consul General Martin, interview by Sifra Lentin. 2015. *History of the Consulate General of Switzerland in Mumbai* (October 23).

Dara Mehta, Aban Davar, interview by Sifra Lentin. 2017. *History of Le Cercle Litteraire* (February-March).

Dwivedi, Sharada, Rahul Mehrotra. 1995. *Bombay: The Cities Within*. Bombay: India Book House.

Edwardes, S.M. 1923. *Memoir of Sir Dinshaw Manockjee Petit, First Baronet, 1823–1901*. England: Frederick Hall at The Oxford University Press.

Ergen, Sabri, interview by Lentin Sifra. 2015. *Turkish Consul General in Mumbai*. Mumbai.

Gangar, Amrit. 2013. *The Music that Still Rings at Dawn, Every Dawn: Walter Kaufmann in India, 1934–1946*. Mumbai: Goethe Institute/Max Muller Bhavan Mumbai.

Glazer, Theresa, Jan Siedlecki, Danka Pniewska, Wiesia Kleszho, Chmielowska. 2002. *Poles in India 1942–1948: Second World War Story*. Warsaw: Association of Poles in India 1942–1948.

Leszek, Consul General of Poland Brenda, interview by Sifra Lentin. 2015. *History of the Consulate General of Poland in Mumbai* (September 24).

Milburn, William. 1813. *Oriental commerce; containing a geographical description of the principal places in East Indies, China, and Japan, with their produce, manufactures, and trade*. Vol. 1. London: Black, Parry & Co.

Perrin, Consul General Yves, interview by Lentin Sifra. 2015. *History of the Consulat General de France a Bombay* (October 6).

n.d. *Switzerland History*. Accessed November 8, 2015. http://www.nationsonline.org/oneworld/History/Switzerland-history.htm (accessed on 8 November 2015).

Index

Note: Page numbers in *italic* refer to figures; those in **bold** refer to tables; page numbers followed by 'n' refer to notes.

Adamson, Alexander 34
Afghan or Pathan community: in blue-collar jobs 72; British Indian North West Frontier Province from 70; cultural identity, protective of 72; dominant tribes 70, 81n14; Pathan's in Hindi film industry 72; Residential Permits (RPs) 71, 81n15; reverse migration, and trades 70
Aga Khan Development Network (AKDN) 51, 61n7
Agency Houses 4, 34–35, 73, 91, 93–96; English 85, 90; European 34; Forbes & Co. and Bruce, Fawcett & Co. 92; Scott, Tate & Adamson 92
Ahmedabad 36
Ali, Haider (Mysore sultans) 20, 27
Alliance Français 112
American Center Library 107
American Civil War (1861–1865) 31
American ice trade 106–107
Amichund, Motichund 34
Anand, Swami 50
Anglo-Burmese War 28, 30; Burmese royal family, exiled in Ratnagiri 31–32; first, 1824–1826 30; third, for teakwook 28, 30–31
Anglo-Mysore Wars, in Deccan 20, 27–28, 39n5

Angre, Kanhoji: 'admiral,' term use 13, 22n8; attack on, Kenery and Kolaba 16; colonial narratives, revised 14; *dastak* (pass) 11, 14, 15; death of, and descendants of 10, 17, 22n10; importance, to Bombay history 14; INS Angre 14; *Pyrate Angria* 13; reign, over North Konkan seas 11, 13; relevance in present, reasons for 14–15; writ of closed seas 11, 13–15
anti-piracy missions 13, 16–17, 25; Peshwa Nanasaheb, role in Angres defeat 14, 17; Royal Navy and Bombay Marine, joint operation 16–17; *see also* piracy, and pirates
anti-slavery treaties 47–48, 84, 87
Awaara film 117

Bagchi, Amiya 91
Baghdadi Jewish merchant community 4, 65–66, 80n2; David Sassoon immigration 66–67, 71, 90; Jews persecution, in Baghdad 66, 81n6; settlements, near synagogue 67–68, 81n7
Baldry, Robert 25
Bank of Bombay, (old, 1840) 93, 94–95
Bank of Madras (1843) 94, 95, 102n3
Bank of Western India 1842: global

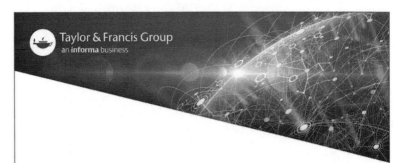

Taylor & Francis eBooks

www.taylorfrancis.com

A single destination for eBooks from Taylor & Francis
with increased functionality and an improved user
experience to meet the needs of our customers.

90,000+ eBooks of award-winning academic content in
Humanities, Social Science, Science, Technology, Engineering,
and Medical written by a global network of editors and authors.

TAYLOR & FRANCIS EBOOKS OFFERS:

A streamlined
experience for
our library
customers

A single point
of discovery
for all of our
eBook content

Improved
search and
discovery of
content at both
book and
chapter level

REQUEST A FREE TRIAL
support@taylorfrancis.com